FRANÇOIS

François

A Memoir

Kyle Thomas Smith

StreetLegal Press

François: A Memoir

Published by StreetLegal Press

Cover art: "Male Nude, with Arms Up-Stretched,"
1828, by William Etty

Library of Congress Control Number: 2023952149

ISBN (paperback): 9781662947551
eISBN: 9781662947568

To the lost and lonely,
May you find direction and love

Please note that although this is a work of nonfiction, many names and some surface details have been changed to protect identities.

"We do not receive wisdom, we must discover it for ourselves, after a journey through the wilderness, which no one else can make for us, which no one can spare us, for our wisdom is the point of view from which we come at last to regard the world."
—Marcel Proust

"People like these were untouchables to me, raised on some other planet and then transplanted into my general vicinity to remind me how bad I was living."
- Junot Díaz, "Boyfriend"

There's an album called *Classical Music for Creativity* that is perfect, or almost perfect, for blocking out noise so you can read, write, or study. I suppose you could paint or draw or sculpt or design clothes to it too. You can buy it on iTunes for $7.99. I could look up the track listings and rattle them off for you, but the truth is, I don't know which track is which, or who composed what, when it's sounding away in my earbuds. All I know is that when I hit shuffle, there are no lyrics and no singing to distract me, and the orchestras' crescendos are often all that it takes to bring what I'm writing to a crescendo.

Theories like the Mozart effect say that just listening to classical music will raise your IQ. That kind of thing used to be hugely important to me when I was younger, but what's more important to me now is that the music drowns out other people's chatter. I don't want anyone or anything intruding on my flow. Still, there's too much cabin fever when you write at home past a certain number of days and libraries are so stuffy. Plus, you can't bring drinks in. So, I go to cafes. I've been going to them ever since I was a teenager. It's good to be around people, and even to hear a dull roar of their voices, just to know you're a part of something larger than yourself and your confines. It's even better if you can tune everybody out when you're around them and for me, *Classical Music for Creativity* does the trick.

In fact, before I go on, I have a little anecdote about this. Once I came home from writing at the Think Coffee that's just around the corner from our apartment and as I was taking off my shoes and putting them on our shoe rack, I saw my teacher Martin coming out of our guest room. Martin stays with us whenever he's in New York. He's British but he lives at the retreat center that he co-founded in the Dordogne region of southwest France almost 30 years ago.

Martin used to go all over the world teaching meditation and dharma. Then the pandemic hit, and Martin caught Covid twice, all the way out in the French countryside. He has long Covid now. It's been a crash course in the insubstantiality of the body and how if death doesn't get you now, it will at some point. Be that as it may, I'm so grateful that he survived. Now he's more inclined to stay home and teach online, so I don't see him in person as much as I used to. I do try to go to his center whenever I can, but time and money don't always permit.

Yet this time he was in town to work on his documentary film on old monks whose teachings have had a subtle but significant impact on contemporary culture, especially Buddhist cultures. He was meeting with some producers whose offices are right across the street from where we live now, just off Union Square. His objective is for us, the audience, to hear the extraordinary, extemporaneous words of these yogis before they die, which isn't bound to be too long from now.

As Martin walked into our hallway, he was carrying a laptop and speakers for the webinar that he was going to be hosting on our terrace.

"Good morning, Martin," I said, "Did you have a good night's sleep? You look all dressed up and ready for the day." Martin looked at me quizzically and said, "Didn't you see me? I went to that cafe and sat right next to you for about 20 minutes." My eyes went wide, "You did?" The café's nine or ten small round white marble tables, which are all stationed above a long, L-shaped brown leather sofa bench, are each spaced only about one foot away from the other. I couldn't imagine that I wouldn't have seen Martin in there, especially if he was sitting right next to me. He said, "I even said, 'Hi, Kyle.' But you didn't look up. You were absolutely riveted to what you were writing."

I apologized profusely. I told him I would have said hello if I'd have known he was there. It's just that *Classical Music for Creativity* was playing, and it always puts me in the zone. He gave me a good-natured chuckle and a "think nothing of it" wave of the hand.

If anybody can understand being in a samadhi state, it's Martin. When he was all of 19, he flew to India with no luggage and nothing but a toothbrush in his pocket. He ended up staying in a sadhu's hermitage near Dharmsala for three years, meditating all day and night, only taking time out to do chores or to go on three-month retreats in Thai monasteries when the law said he had to be out of the country to renew his visa. The sadhu was Hindu and Martin's practice was Buddhist, yet the sadhu didn't mind that in the least. He simply encouraged Martin to go deep into his practice. It was the start of Martin's dharma career—if you want to call dharma a career. It's more of a vocation, a ministry.

I once told Martin that what he was doing in the Himalayas in his twenties is what I was doing in my notebooks throughout my twenties. That's probably a stretch, but looking back, I wonder if it's that much of one? After I found the writing practice of Natalie Goldberg, who has been a Zen student for over fifty years and a writing teacher for about as long and who had long ago devised a free-writing practice that is consonant with Zen practice, I spent a good 12 years filling up notebooks all day, every day with my discursive thoughts, all according to her method, thinking I would come out the other side of it as the next Steinbeck. The Steinbeck part didn't happen, but the focus and determination did.

And when the iPhone came out, I could finally retire the cruddy, cushiony Walgreens earplugs that I used to wear while writing in cafes. Now I could listen to music on slick AirPods.

Jazz works fine, it has a beatnik-y jive, but classical lends itself to high drama, which is more my jam.

The problem with Apple Music's classical playlist is that there's too much opera on it, so I have to keep pressing the right arrow until I land on something instrumental. Now, the good thing about opera is that it's rarely in English so the lyrics won't get in the way of the words you're trying to put on paper or on screen (unlike everybody else, I don't usually use a computer until I'm at the final drafts of a project). English-language writers probably have an easier time writing to opera than Italian or French or German writers do, but the booming voices can overpower an anglophone's ability to concentrate too. Also, there are too many pauses during recitatives. That's when the ragged voices of coffeehouse customers can barge in and throw you off. But there are no pregnant pauses or droning baritones or squalling sopranos on *Classical Music for Creativity*, so that's my go-to album.

It wasn't enough to mute everyone around me yesterday, though.

I was writing at Claudette. That's the Provençal-style restaurant, up the street from Washington Square, with the blue gingham tablecloths. If I go there at all, I go toward the end of the lunch shift when there are more tables available and when I can be sure that I'm not taking up too much space. I don't order lunch. I only order a coffee and some pumpkin bread, but I tip at about the same amount as the bill, so the servers don't mind me being there. Yesterday two middle-aged women were sitting at the table next to mine, still having lunch. There was an extended beat of sound as *Classical Music for Creativity* switched tracks and it was in that interval that I heard one of the women, the one seated opposite me (albeit at the other table), whimper.

I looked up but quickly looked back down at my notebook when our eyes met. I resumed scribbling a lot of gibberish. Her friend was there to comfort her. She didn't need me butting in and asking her what was wrong. I did see that she had wiped tears from her left eye, though. I pretended to keep writing so she wouldn't feel like she was making a scene. I hit pause on *Classical Music for Creativity*, though, so I could eavesdrop.

Her friend, a matronly woman with a soft froth of short white curls, was wearing an elegant diamond on the ring finger of her left hand. She patted her dining companion's wrist as her companion struggled to pull herself back together. The companion had no rings on her fingers, although her nails were nicely manicured and polished to a tasteful red gleam. She also appeared to be at least ten years younger than the white-haired woman.

"Now, Linda," the older woman said as her companion took a few sips of water to contain herself and keep from hyperventilating,

"Let's take a step back and review this. You walked off with a lot of stock. You have an ample 401(k). You've been saving responsibly throughout the years. You have the healthiest savings account of anyone I know, and speaking of 'healthiest,' you have your health. That's not nothing. Believe me, I know. And they've given you 18 months of Cobra before you'll have to purchase an independent health insurance. You have only one property, your apartment, so you're not over-leveraged, and you've almost paid off your mortgage. Add to this that you have a pension, and they gave you an extremely generous severance package. You're set for life. You could even, I don't know, take up knitting! And do nothing but that for the rest of your life, and you'd be fine. Even if you never sell a hat or a sweater. I'm joking. But you know what I mean. You're in the catbird seat. This was a blessing."

"I'm not ready," Linda broke down, wiping her eyes, where the mascara had blurred, but not obscenely, "I mean, I know I hated the long hours and having no life. But this *was* my life."

"And now a new life awaits you, a fuller life," the older woman said, her eyes sagacious and focused, her fingers steepled under her chin and over her frisée salad.

"About ten years too soon," said the younger woman.

"But Linda, the writing was on the wall," the older woman told her, "It's been on the wall for years. How many times have you told me, 'I'm getting expensive. People in senior management are dropping like flies in a napalm storm.' Your words, Linda."

"I know," said Linda, "I always knew it was a possibility. But I always thought...this is ridiculous...but I always thought that if I stayed on my guard and always mentioned to myself, and to you, and to my sister, that the threat was always standing in the shadows, that then the threat would know that I was on to it and it'd skip past me and find someone who didn't see it coming. I thought I could ward off the threat if I just worried enough."

"Is it a threat or a blessing?" the older woman asked.

"I don't know what else to do with myself," Linda said, "This is what I've always done."

"You didn't ever foresee a time when you'd retire?" the older woman asked.

"Of course, I did. That's why I have the 401(k). And another I.R.A. But ten years down the road. Not now. This hit me upside the head. I know it shouldn't have. But it did. I'm not even 60. Not until next year."

"Could you work somewhere else?"

"Headhunters have called me. There's stuff out there. But... This is going to sound insane."

"Try me."

Linda put her hands over her eyes, "Okay, you know I'm not one of those people. I don't run around wearing crystals and... doing whatever it is *those* people do...although I might find out what they do sooner than I think at the rate I'm going...But something in my gut just curls up like a fist. And just like a fist, it pounds on me from the inside whenever a headhunter calls—"

"Have you seen a doctor?"

"No!" Linda said, shaking her head and cringing, "I'm not explaining this right. It's not a literal fist. It's not a literal pain. It's just an...insistence," she took a deep breath, "An insistence that I leave the industry and do something else entirely. Even if it's nothing. I...I filled out a volunteer application with the ASPCA so I could help with the dogs and cats."

"Good!"

"They said there's a six-month waitlist for volunteer positions," she took a sip of water and leaned forward intently, "They say they'll call when they're ready for me. They asked if I'd like to adopt a dog or a cat in the meantime. I've always wanted one. One of each. I just never had the time. That's what I said about dating too. And children. But they've seen my application for volunteering. They seem to think I'd make a good owner too. Maybe that should be my first order of business while I wait for their volunteer coordinator to call."

"I think your first order of business should be to relax," the older woman said, "Otherwise you're going to drive that poor dog and cat crazy." They both laughed, especially Linda, who laughed uproariously, bucking back and forth like a bronco rider, in the way that only those who could really use a laugh do. The older woman continued, "I think you should travel first. And now what I'm going to do is I'm going to ask for the check and I'm going to pick up it up—*no, no, no, I absolutely insist.* — And we're going to go to my place and we're going to have dessert there. I have a scrumptious lemon meringue pie. And then I'm going to give you the keys to our place in Umbria."

"Where's that?" asked Linda.

"In Italy," she said, "You know, where we stay at least half the year."

"Oh, your villa!"

"Yes," said the older woman, "And I'm not going to release you from my custard-y lemon meringue custody until after I see you get on my computer and book your ticket. How long has it been since you had a vacation?" Linda began to answer but the older woman interrupted, "Family funerals and palliative care visits don't count."

Linda guffawed, "Well, then I can't even remember offhand." Linda took a deep breath, "Thank you. A vacation does sound like just what the doctor ordered, but it also sounds like a band-aid solution. What am I supposed to do when I get back?"

"You can let that question marinate in marinara sauce while you're savoring the most delicious calamari you've ever set your teeth to," said the older woman, "You might come back and decide that your new hobby is learning Italian. Maybe over here at NYU. And the ASPCA is going to call you one day. Just don't sit by the phone waiting. A watched phone never rings, at least never with the call you want. And when you get back, you'll book an appointment to adopt a dog and a cat, and they'll keep you busy. And who knows, you might meet somebody."

"Not if I'm a crazy cat lady," said Linda.

"You'll have a dog too," the older woman said, "That'll get you out. On walks. You might even meet Mr. Right at the dog park over here. Or even if you just got a cat. There are crazy cat daddies out there too, you know. My Leo has become one with our Glockenspiel ever since he retired. Oh, Glockenspiel is our white angora, you'll meet her at our place. Leo even showed me a cat-daddies website. It's adorable. I don't think it's a dating site, though. But you never know. These days there might be one just for that."

"Well, let's not get ahead of ourselves here," Linda said, pushing her palms out.

"You're right, you're right," the older woman said, "I'm sorry. One thing at a time. But a word to the wise: Somebody told me before I retired that I would have to have eight hobbies if I wanted to keep my marbles. I took that to heart. It keeps me sane. But you'll have time to figure that out in Italy. Come, let's get the check."

They settled up. I turned the music back on. I saw a title roll past on my iPhone screen: Now I was on to some movement or other of *The Brandenburg Concertos*, I can't remember which one.

I went back to writing. Before I reached the end of the next page, the two women had left to book Linda's flight.

Before I closed the notebook, I opened to a new page, where I wrote out a *metta* (loving-kindness) blessing, the kind I normally send with my legs crossed on a zafu cushion and my eyelids at half-mast, but there was no way to do this inconspicuously on the booth cushion at Claudette, so I did it stealth with a pen and paper: "May Linda be happy/May Linda be at peace/May Linda live with ease of well-being/May Linda be well loved," and lastly, I wrote, "May Linda fully enjoy Italy."

❧

ast night, I saw a meme. It was a doctored Roy Lichtenstein cartoon where a man in glasses says to a woman in a pink business suit jacket, "You look tired." The woman says, "Thanks. I stayed up all night obsessing about things I have no control over."

I turned off my phone and went to bed.

My husband Julius turned out the light on his nightstand when he saw that I'd fallen asleep.

I wasn't asleep for long, though. These days, I almost never am. It could have something to do with the fact that I normally have to move my legs but find that our gray cat Giacomo and our black cat Fiorello, who both sleep on my legs when I'm in bed, have long turned to dead weight and I'm stuck.

We named Giacomo after Giacomo Puccini, one of Julius's favorite opera composers, and we named Fiorello after Café Fiorello, the restaurant where we usually meet up for dinner after Julius goes to the opera at Lincoln Center. Julius has been an opera aficionado ever since he was a little boy, growing up in San Juan. His grandfather, a gentleman of leisure, owned an actual warehouse full of opera 45's and would spend his mornings listening to them in his silk robe with a glass of scotch in his hand. Julius didn't inherit his grandfather's money, but he did inherit his taste. Opera is too slow and stilted for me, so I usually go to the café area at Shakespeare & Company and write there unless Julius absolutely insists that I sit through one of those lachrymose molasses marathons at the Met with him.

At night, I never want to disturb Giacomo and Fiorello's sleep, though, which is funny because they have no qualms about disturbing mine, so instead I just lay there. And it's strange how, for all the meditating I've done and all the retreats I've gone on over the past 26 years, I forget all about present-moment awareness as I lay prone in the witching hours. If I'm not perseverating over my countless past failures and regrets, I'm obsessing over what other people are doing or have done or could be doing with their lives.

Even a total stranger like Linda, whose life is none of my business, soon becomes a subject of obsession for me. Did she book the ticket? I wondered. Or did she find a way to get out of going? Did she choose the path of least resistance, as most people do, and call a headhunter so she can hold her wrists out for a new pair of golden shackles because there's nothing scarier than freedom?

Or is she going to break free like those women in movies like *Shirley Valentine*; *Muriel's Wedding*; *Eat, Pray, Love*; and *How Stella Got Her Groove Back*?

Or will Linda get sick and die because deep down she feels she has no purpose anymore?

Eventually I brought myself back to the present moment and started sending Linda more *metta* instead of insisting that she go the more adventurous route, "May Linda be happy/May Linda be at peace…," the kind of blessings I'd started sending her in my notebook at Claudette.

But then I thought, What was up with those eight hobbies that that white-haired woman was talking about?

It sounded like an awful lot to keep track of. She said the eight hobbies, whatever they were, were enough to help her keep her sanity. They sounded like more than enough to make me lose mine.

Even if Linda could come up with eight hobbies, I wondered, could they ever be enough to keep her mind off the distinction she had undoubtedly enjoyed before her company strapped the golden parachute on her back and gave her the heave-ho? When she's cleaning up puppy puddles and scooping up kitty litter in cages at the ASPCA, will she miss the prestige she once had?

I wouldn't know. I've never had much prestige myself. I did used to covet other people's prestige, though, when I was much younger.

My astrologer says it's because I have a Capricorn moon, but he says that people with my moon placement tend to care less about these things as they get older, so long as they start to give themselves the love and approval that they'd hoped the world would have given them. Otherwise, they just stay lost and deluded.

He's right, I've found.

♋

My name is Kyle Smith. I also go by my author's name, Kyle Thomas Smith, which is also the name I was given at birth. I use my full name to distinguish myself from another New York writer whose name is also Kyle Smith. That Kyle Smith is far more famous than I am or ever will be. He writes for *The New York Post* and *The Wall Street Journal*. All you have to do is read his articles and the papers he writes for to see that his politics lean right. If you've ever read anything by me, though, you'll see pretty immediately that mine lean left. Another difference between him and me is that he's married to a woman, and I'm married to a man.

My saving grace is that I married well, in every way. It's the subject of my most recent book, *Cockloft: Scenes from a Gay Marriage*, a cross-genre humor memoir whose title essay explores the hell that broke loose when a squirrel invaded our house in Brooklyn. I promised Julius I wouldn't make him the subject of this book, however.

Julius does deserve a word, though. Julius is a successful attorney, mostly specializing in compliance. I'm a freelance and creative writer. And just so I can beat you to the punch about my spanking white, privileged ass, I will also admit to being a childless househusband who got to ditch my day jobs after only a year into our 17-year relationship. We used to live in that squirrel-ransacked house I mentioned, in the Park Slope neighborhood of Brooklyn. Then, as is also mentioned toward the end of *Cockloft*, Julius stopped working for the banks and we moved to San Francisco, where he got a job in tech.

We spent four years in San Francisco. I became heavily involved in something like five different *sanghas* (Buddhist communities) as Julius became immersed in his new industry. Then came the pandemic. All the meditation centers and all the offices closed their physical spaces. Thank God neither one of us got Covid. Sure, we were extra careful with masks and social distancing but so were a lot of other people who still ended up getting it, Martin being only one example. Lockdown in San Francisco gave us pause to see that we'd left our hearts in New York. All our all-night conversations seemed to revolve around how much we missed home, so we went through the headache of selling our condo in a buyer's market. It finally sold in January 2022, and we promptly vacated. We had managed to secure a multi-year lease from the tenants who are renting our house in Brooklyn, so we can't move back to the house yet. In the meantime, we're renting an apartment in downtown Manhattan, right across the street from the New School.

We'll be in Manhattan for some time, which is fine by us. We're enjoying ourselves. During the pandemic, we had both put on pandemic weight, which we worked off by buying Fitbits and walking all over the Bay Area. Now that we're back in New York, we've established the habit of walking everywhere we go in the city. Even if we have appointments way the hell uptown or tickets to shows at Brooklyn Academy of Music, we walk there. As a result, we're in the best shape of our lives. We only take the subway if we're really pressed for time. Otherwise, we each use our own two feet and are constantly surprised to see that an address that seemed so far away did not rack up the amount of miles we thought it would on our watches because everything is so close in New York, especially compared to cities and towns where you're forced to drive everywhere. Plus, we've switched to Apple Watches, which are nowhere near as generous with step and calorie-burn counts as Fitbit, though Apple Watches may be more honest.

One place that is especially close to us is my Buddhist center, New York Insight. I used to take a 45-minute-to-one-hour subway ride to it, at least twice a week, when we lived in Park Slope. The center that NYI had for decades on 27th St closed during lockdown and they're currently looking for a permanent space. Now we live just around the corner from its temporary meeting place at Still Mind Zendo, whose space NYI rents when the zendo isn't hosting its own programs.

New York Insight recently asked me to become a practice leader and a teacher. I was floored. I mean, I'd been practicing with them for about 20 years, even when I had to do so online from San Francisco, and I'd even gotten certified to teach meditation and dharma about ten years ago through Martin's Mindfulness Institute, which was then based in the UK but has since moved its operations to France and California. Yet back then NYI had a teacher's council that was chock-a-block with senior teachers, so I never did anything with my certification and was more than happy to just remain a student and a dedicated practitioner for the rest of my life. But most of their senior teachers stepped down after 2020 and the center needed new blood, so they asked me if I'd step up. Despite my fears of not being up to the task, I said yes.

And then I panicked during a zoom meeting I had about all this with Martin. I said that if given enough time to prepare, I could probably work up a good dharma talk. I've certainly sat through enough of them to know the formula. But I told him I was petrified of being caught flat-footed when it'd come time for students to ask me questions about their practice, which most often leads to them asking the teacher questions about what they should do about their most vexing problems or about how they should be living their lives. What the hell do I know about how they should live their lives? Who am I to say?

I said to Martin, "I read all these dharma books, and I read all about these Tibetan rinpoches who become homeless mendicants in Nepal, just so they can deepen their practice. And you did something similar in India when you were starting out. One guy I was on retreat with had been a monk in Burma for five years. Many others have spent six months or a year, or even more, at the Thai Forest Refuge.—I'm this neurotic, bougie gay guy living in New York. What the hell do I have to teach?"

Martin answered, "The dharma of a neurotic, bougie gay guy living in New York."

In other words, not everything has to be done with a shaved head, robes, and an alms bowl. It takes all kinds to make a sangha, and it takes all kinds of teachers too. This is what Martin was trying to communicate to me, and he offered to mentor me on an ongoing basis. I'm so glad. I know he knows what he's doing, even if he didn't when he first stepped off the plane in India. I'm going on a retreat at his center in France next month. He and I will talk more about this when we have face time.

I've been to Nepal but never to India, except for once when the plane we were taking from Bangkok to Bhutan made an unexpected stopover at a remote Indian airport where it picked up Richard Gere and a couple of his lama friends. Julius got his movie stars mixed up and said, "Hey look! There's Warren Beatty." Eh, at least he got the generation right…kind of.

While in Nepal, Julius and I visited Lumbini, where the Buddha was born. It was there that I arranged to meet with Venerable Metteyya, a fetching young Buddhist monk, now in his late thirties, whom I'd also met when he'd come to speak at New

York Insight. Metteyya had been born into a wealthy, supremely educated Brahmin family before he converted to Buddhism and became a renunciate. He built and now runs a girls' school, The Metta School, that teaches young girls from Lumbini how to read and write. The school also teaches them home economics so that they can become efficient householders, as well as other trades so that they can qualify for government jobs and become empowered outside the home, something that doesn't often happen in a region where girls are expected to become wives and mothers by their early teens and where the literacy rate hovers at around 20%. Even basic skills that the school teaches like boiling water could prevent dysentery and sundry other diseases that claim an inordinate number of lives in Lumbini. We took a tour of the Metta School and met some of the girls who live there. Just meeting them I could see that the Buddha was not the last impressive being to come out of Lumbini, and The Metta School is there to ensure that there will be many more where he came from. Thanks in part to Metteyya, Nepal's future will be female.

Julius and I do plan to go to India next year for my fiftieth birthday. I checked with my astrologer, and he says it would be an excellent idea for me to spend it in Bodhgaya. That's where the Buddha achieved his awakening over 2,600 years ago. So that's where we plan on being on my birthday, provided Julius can get off work.

It might even make me a better teacher. It made the Buddha a better one. In fact, he didn't even become the Buddha until he went there and sat under the bodhi tree for 49 days. And then he got up, dusted himself off, and went off and taught the dharma for 45 years. Who knows how going there might empower me as I begin teaching at New York Insight.

I first learned about Buddhism in religion class at the Jesuit high school I went to in Chicago, but that lesson only lasted one or two class periods. Still, it was enough to plant a seed. I didn't start meditating or reading books about Buddhism until I went through a crisis in my early twenties, though—but more on that later.

$\mathscr{O}$

Our house in Brooklyn is an old limestone, built in 1901. It needs a lot of renovations done on it once our tenants' lease is up. That may mean that we can't live in it for still more years, so we may have to keep renting an apartment as the house undergoes overhaul. Julius is eyeing retirement, though, and he says that if a certain deal goes through at work, we might be able to cash in our chips and move to Paris while the house is being rehabbed.

Now, my French is terrible, as certain members of the French public have made a point of pointing out. Whenever I go there, people cut me off and just answer me in English before I can even finish my sentence. I still take French classes, though, and my best friend Sébastien, a dharma brother whom I met in San Francisco, is from France and he helps me out. And I'm going on a one-week retreat at Martin's center in Dordogne next month and it will all be conducted in French. It won't be enough to make me fluent, but it will give me a taste of total immersion.

I don't know if I'll ever become fluent. Still, wouldn't it be lovely to live in Paris?

♋

I thought about that a lot in the dead of night, last night. It was just one of those things that creeps into your head and won't let go. Accordion music kept sounding in my mind, and I practically hallucinated the sight of winding cobblestone streets and balconies with wrought-iron rims and wide-open French doors, ornamented with billowing white curtains. And then I finally fell asleep. And then the cats woke me up at about 5:15, pawing at my nose and chin. So, I woke up, fed them, and got on with my day.

I did my morning writing. I said my morning prayers. I did half an hour of morning meditation and then worked out on our elliptical machine for an hour and ten minutes. That's where I also do the Ray Bradbury Trio. Ray Bradbury told his students to read one poem, one essay, and one short story a day for 1,000 days. It was supposed to help them become better writers. I'm about eight months into it. I read all these things on my phone while I work out. I read one Shakespeare sonnet, one "Poem of the Day" from poetryfoundation.org (today's was "Ode to a Large Tuna in the Market" by Pablo Neruda), and usually a dharma essay that, I hope, will prepare me to teach, as well as a short story from any number of anthologies. Today's installment was from *The Complete Stories of Guy de Maupassant*—that anthology alone could take one thousand days— and it was called "An Adventure in Paris." It's about a provincial woman who sneaks off to the capital and has an affair with a distinguished man of letters, only to find that, for all his cachet, he leaves her cold.

I took a shower after my workout. Later, as I brushed my teeth at the sink, I watched a talk that had popped up on the YouTube app on my phone. It was all about "re-owning the projection." What the presenter meant by that was that we're so quick to ascribe godhead, or even just good qualities, to people we admire, or to people we have a crush on, and yet we're so reluctant to acknowledge that we may have these same qualities, or commensurate ones, inside ourselves. I can see that I've done this several times already, up to this point in the book. I've gone on at length about how Julius and Martin and Metteyya and the Buddha and Guy de Maupassant are such remarkable polymaths where I find it a wonder that I even manage to get from one day to the next.

I'm not the only one who has ever felt this way about themself either. I saw that the talk I was watching had garnered hundreds of thousands of views and tens of thousands of comments. I read some of the comments as I completed my ablutions. Almost all the ones I read were bite-sized tales of hero worship: a neophyte meets a mentor or lover who, for a time, seems to walk on clouds until the clouds inevitably part and expose their feet of clay, at which point the nonpareil falls from the sky and comes crashing down to earth.

I wanted to chime in about my experience with François, but I had no idea how to put it all into a YouTube comment box. Plus, any honest accounting of my own endless ineptitude, especially where François was concerned, would surely have attracted the attention of trolls and I didn't want those creeps ruining my day. I'm the first to admit that at no point in my life have I ever been anywhere near as competent as Linda, the lady at Claudette, and this was especially true when I knew François. And François wasn't even anywhere near as available as Linda's mentor, the woman with the short, curly white hair, who spends half her year in Italy.

Now that I'm about to turn 50, I'm inclined to ask myself, why bother saying anything about someone I knew for such a short period of time? Then I considered that I was young when I met François, and these encounters are big deals when we're young—catalytic even. They have an immeasurable impact on our lives going forward.

So, once I was done brushing my teeth, I spit the toothpaste out, wiped the foam off my mouth, and resolved to forgo the comment boxes.

If I really needed to get the story off my chest, why not just put it all into a Word doc? So, that's what I'm doing now.

⅁

I was 23 and was about four months out of college, working as an office temp in Chicago. I'd worked for lawyers pretty much all through college, but only as a file clerk and a copy boy. The secretaries were my buffer when any of the big guys were in a rage and needed someone to take it out on. Who were they going to aim for first? The copy boy/file clerk? Not when there's a perfectly good secretary sitting there, one who has dependents at home and a job she can't afford to lose. In those days, I could just stand there and file or photocopy and let my mind go off and fantasize about the life I was going to have after college.

I knew I wanted to be an author. I knew it would be a steep climb with no guarantee of success, but I thought the gods would decide at last to shine on me since they'd given me such a shitty childhood and adolescence, full of bullying and family and peer rejection over my not being like other guys, and over my liking other guys. The gods owed me big for that, I thought. Still, I wanted to be somewhat realistic about this. I had read about the *La Bohème* lives of so many of the authors and artists we studied in school. I thought I was going to have to live their lives if I was going to earn my stripes. I'd have to keep living in slummy apartments and working exhausting day jobs and every night after work, I thought I'd have to go home and punch another clock for the long night of writing ahead. That's what Tennessee Williams used to do. He'd work at the shoe factory, come home, fix himself a pot of coffee, and go to his typewriter. Sooner or later, his body would give out and his typewriter would become his iron pillow. He'd wake up the next morning with all his clothes still on from the day before, the typewriter keys embossed on the side of his face.

I had no idea where I was going to fit a relationship into any of this. But I was raised Catholic and though I'd left the Church, it has a way of never leaving you. And it made it clear that gay love was strictly prohibited. Now, I'd step out and have my flings from time to time. Yet one of the greatest shames of my life was that I was also imbibing on the work and crackpot theories of Camille Paglia, a hard-ass, über-contrarian provocateur who said that celibacy is a definite option and that some of the best art derives from those who channel their sexual energy into art, not sex, and certainly not into relationships. Part of me always suspected, though, that beneath her rebel façade, there was a recovering Catholic who hadn't quite let go of the strictures and dogmas that she and I were both raised with[1].

This was true of me too. I can see now that I was still trying to find, in my head and in my heart, a compromise between what my parents had taught me and what I truly felt inside. But how do you find a compromise with a father who mocked Black people and Black English and who, after he retired, would spend his afternoons cheering on the ravings of Rush Limbaugh, and who championed Pat Buchanan even though he, my father, had gay offspring? How do you compromise with a mother who was constantly threatening white flight from the neighborhood you grew up in, and who told you she thinks AIDS patients should be sent to leper colonies, and who, when you came out and then told her that there is strong evidence of a genetic link to homosexuality, told you that if homosexuality were genetic, they would have found a way to screen it out of the population? I hated them

---

1   In François Ozon's 2003 film *Swimming Pool*, the gamy antagonist Julie (Ludivine Sagnier) tells the crime-novelist protagonist (Charlotte Rampling) that she, the crime novelist, "writes about dirty things but never does them." That, to me, describes Camille Paglia in a nutshell. Paglia said that her objective in writing her magnum opus *Sexual Personae: Art and Decadence from Nefertiti to Emily Dickinson* (1990) was "to please no one and to offend everyone…I try to zap it with pornographic intensity." She has also publicly stated that she had no sex life for most of the twenty years that it took to write the manifesto. Comparing herself to Jean Genet, who wrote his first novel *Our Lady of the Flowers* (1949) while incarcerated, Paglia went on to say, "It took all the resources of being Catholic to cut myself off and sit in my cell," when she was writing what she calls her "prison book."

both for espousing and airing these views and for encouraging my much older siblings to ridicule and verbally and physically abuse me for opposing them both. I hated them for weaponizing their religion against me when I came out and for sticking to their guns, believing they'd be rewarded for it at the pearly gates, instead of empathizing and accepting me. Both my parents died, one right after the other, ten years ago, and what makes me sad is that I have never once missed them, and I have had no relationship with my siblings for decades. And yet, in my late teens and early twenties, I felt such crippling sex guilt that I decided I would throw myself into becoming a better writer instead of getting into relationships and experiencing life. As Thomas Mann wrote in *Tonio Kröger*, "You can either live or write." And I rationalized that such self-abnegation would make me a literary sensation like my sexually tormented heroes, Tennessee Williams, Gerard Manley Hopkins, Virginia Woolf, Yukio Mishima, and of course Thomas Mann.

Now, I hear you. None of that sounds like a life anyone would want. But the day that all your hard work pays off does—all that hard work you put in during all those lonely, sexless nights at home. The day you get your big break does. The day you cash your first gargantuan royalty check does. The day you can march into your boss's office and tell them where they can stick their job does.

The day you get to move to Paris does.

And even back then, in the nineties, there were a whole lot of books on the market that said you could "vision" your way into your dream life. So, all this fame and renown were going to happen eventually, weren't they? After all, I was visioning up a storm.

And I haunted the arthouses and rented up all the international films I could from Facets Multimedia. I saw myself living a life worthy of being captured in a grainy, black-and-white Jean-Luc Godard movie.

Now, having said all that I've said about living on the margins, I was also starting to feel that, now that I had a degree, I should probably get a job that'd pay me more than I was making at my student job. And for all the artistic integrity the bad-ass part of me thought I ought to live up to, I couldn't help but notice that other people my age were starting to work quote-unquote real jobs and living much better as a result.

After graduation, I had enough law office experience on my résumé to become an administrative assistant and from there, I began telling myself, I could work my way up the ranks. "I can always do my writing on the side," I said. Not six months before, I would have called this selling out. Now I was calling it growing up.

And so, I registered with an employment agency, and they set me up for an interview to become the administrative assistant for the chief legal counsel at a humanitarian organization. The chief legal counsel didn't want to hire me, but I was young and cute with a snappy epicene wit that somehow charmed his colleagues, and he was outvoted after my final interview. He straight-up told me so on my first day. From there, he set out on a campaign of browbeating and bullying, leering and scoffing whenever he'd pass my desk. My new coworkers would tell me about all the secretaries he'd chased out before me and how he was even trying to get people fired who didn't even work in his department, just because he'd decided he didn't like them. Since they'd revealed to me the shapes of things to come, I walked out on the job after only one week. It served as a cautionary tale that I'd have to pay heed to years later, in my work with other nonprofits: Just because someone sits high atop a humanitarian organization doesn't mean they're a humanitarian themself, or even remotely humane. Maybe they're in it for the prestige. Whatever their reason for being there, it's best to go in with your eyes open.

Having walked out so soon from my first job, I was forced to temp until I could find something perm. And all that I had on my résumé were law-office jobs, so the temp agency gave me a spot in the law office of a for-profit hospital. The words "for-profit hospital" alone should tell you that this organization was the opposite of humanitarian. I was, in other words, sent to work for an office that defended price-gouging. The hospital jacked up the rates on treatments, services, and meds and then pocketed the difference. Add to this that all the legal counsel's office had in the way of décor were sickly yellow walls and slate gray filing cabinets. My job during college had been a civil-service job but we'd at least had prints on the walls of *Starry Night*, *The Lady of Shallot*, and a still life of a pot of violets. Why couldn't the law office of a for-profit hospital put at least that much on their walls? They had the money. Were they anti-art? It was probably a safe bet, given the level of sensitivity it takes to add surcharges to healthcare. Still, a job is a job, and rent was due on the first of the month. I went to work there.

There was only one other person in the office besides me. She was a fifty-year-old attorney named Anne. Even as I count the years that have come and gone since then, it's hard for me to believe that Anne was only a year older than I am now.

As I filed medical records, bills, and correspondences away on my first day, Anne and I got to talking. I asked if we'd ever met before, she looked so familiar. She said she didn't think we had, but she said that people had told her that she had the kind of red hair and Irish face that people could have sworn they'd seen at Tim Finnegan's, or was it John Barleycorn's, or was it Somebody O'Other's wake or funeral? I said, "I'm Irish." She asked how many kids were in my family. I said seven. She said, "Sounds Irish enough. What are their names?" I said, "Colleen, Kerry, Kathleen, Kevin, Keith, Kent, and then there's me, Kyle. Oh, and once we had a cat named Kelly." And she remarked on all the "k" sounds, even in the name Colleen, as most people do. She asked where I fell in the birth order. I said, "I'm the youngest. I was a surprise." She said, "Yes, most large families have surprises." Anne said she knew another Irish family who was also given to alliteration when naming children. Anne said, "They have four girls: Melissa, Michaela, Meagan, Molly."

All these names sounded so familiar. I gave a start, "Not Molly McGrory?"

She said, "Yes!"

It just so happened that Molly McGrory and I had gone to the same Jesuit college prep school on the south side of Chicago. It's one of the top-ranking high schools in the state. I don't know about now, but back then, you had to have a 98% on the entrance exam to get in. I didn't have a 98. I got a 65. Nonetheless, the day before acceptance and rejection letters were due to go out, the head priest called me on the phone to personally welcome me to the school. I was a six-time legacy after all and my dad, a worker's compensation attorney, was doing a lot of pro-bono work for the priest, so I was in like Flynn. That was the good news—for me anyway, not for the kid who got bumped because of me.

The bad news was that, after I was accepted, I was expected to *perform* at the level of kids who got 98 and up. It was a sink-or-swim situation. I was a dyslexic kid with severe ADD (undiagnosed on both counts, until my thirties) and a raging gay identity crisis (diagnosed in real time by all the assholes and siblings who ever bullied me). From the first day of freshman year, I sank, hard and fast. I was handed failing grade after failing grade, but somehow (let's be real here, it was because of my family's good standing in the alumni club and all the free legal work my dad was doing for the priest) I always managed to hang on by my fingernails.

I graduated at the rock bottom of the class, though.

On the upside, so did Honoré de Balzac and Émile Zola at their lycées. And I clung to that scrap of trivia for dear life from the time I decided to become a writer at age 15.

Now, I hadn't wanted to become a writer because of any love of literature.

The first time I'd even thought about becoming a writer was when my mother found the title of a geography report that I'd written in sixth grade. We were supposed to choose a country and write about its climate, economy, national pastimes—the basics—and I chose Ireland because that's where my grandparents were from. I titled my report, "Ireland: Land of Hardship, Heartbreak, and Pride." The thing was, I was pretty sure my mother wouldn't like this title. Now, I knew she wouldn't have had much of a problem with the word "hardship" as it has resonance with the character-building Christian motif of the crosses we bear. I knew that pride of nation was another idea she could leap up and salute. But the word "heartbreak" is so often associated with romance and romance is a kissing cousin of S-E-X and my mother, who had been the chair of the Altar & Rosary Society at St. Mary of the Woods, was the fiercest opponent of any discussion of the matter. That's why I relished coming up with the third to last word of the subtitle. I thought it'd scandalize her. Only, when she saw it emblazoned in stenciled letters above a map of Ireland that I'd traced on the cover and colored in with shamrock-green crayon, she had the exact opposite reaction. She gasped, "I…I think you have a future as a writer!" As I was barely passing my classes, even back in sixth grade, I thought, "Ah, a future! I've been wanting one of those." At both school and home, I was constantly being told that a future was something my life was in grave danger of lacking. Now I was being told that a future could be mine if I were to take up writing. So, I began to flirt with the idea.

Now, by the time I finally resolved to make writing my vocation, it was 1989 and I was beginning my sophomore year of high school. I had read only a handful of books by then, if even that many. But what sealed the deal between writing and me was that I would pass through the Logan Square, Bucktown, and Wicker Park neighborhoods of Chicago on the El train to school every day. At the time, these were mostly lower-income, Latinx neighborhoods where white artists had been moving in for the cheap rents. A lot of leather-clad punks with multicolored hair and artists in renegade rags would step on, bearing portfolios, on their ways to their studios or art-school classes. My daily commute became my own personal neo-Weimar cabaret, twice a day.

I couldn't paint or draw or play an instrument, but even the teachers who were most hostile to me in grade school and high school were often forced to concede at parent-teacher conferences that somehow—they had no idea how—I had a flair for writing. I reasoned that creative writing would be a career alternative, and that even if I did get kicked out of high school, all I had to do was write some kick-ass shit that would go over big with publishers and audiences, and that would beat any diploma or Harvard degree all the hell. So, I went full-bore into writing turgid little stories and journal entries, and I started reading voraciously so that I could become a better writer with a better future. I would go to the library and check out the titles of all the classics I'd see on display on the shelves of smoke-filled boho coffeehouses. With the aid of Webster's Dictionary, I read as many of the books on those shelves as I could muster up the will power to read and they began to subtly work on me, especially the novels of D.H. Lawrence. My grades had gone to pot, but that didn't matter. I was under the tutelage of D.H. Lawrence.

Now, Molly McGrory saw something in me when most people didn't. Depression and suicidal ideation, brought on by home and school and abject failure, had taken me to deep, dark places inside myself, places I fear to tread even today as a dedicated practitioner of meditation[2]. My unabated gloom had sensitized me to the point that I started seeking more and more consolation and enlightenment in music, books, movies, and art, but never in drugs. My look was a mashup of the ragbag of mutineers I used to study as I'd skulk around the gutter punks on Belmont and Clark or the *nouveau pauvre* iconoclasts around the Coyote Building or the skell beatniks spewing their Bukowski-esque invectives at open mics at No Exit Café[3]. I was constantly getting pulled into

2   I was recently in Macclesfield, England, visiting the gravestone of Ian Curtis, frontman of the band Joy Division. I'd also stood outside his home, where he'd hanged himself at age 23 on May 18, 1980, the night before Joy Division was due to embark on their make-or-break North American tour. (After Curtis's death, the band soon re-formed under the name New Order, which gradually developed an electronic dance sound that took the club scene by storm, signaling a marked departure from Joy Division's punk-inspired art rock. Although deeply saddened by Curtis's suicide and initially uncertain about what their future would be without him, New Order soon staked their claim on the pantheon of alternative music acts.) As a teenager, I would listen to Joy Division nonstop, unperturbed by Curtis's haunting poetry and low rumbling baritone, all of which reflect the mental state of a young man whose anxiety demon wanted him dead. It had been reflective of my mental state as well, only at the time, I thought Curtis was barely skimming the surface of my own slough of despond. My threshold for willful suffering is no longer anywhere near as high as it had been in the days when Molly McGrory and I were first becoming acquainted.

3   No Exit was a musty café and art gallery, crammed to the gills with used books, in Rogers Park—a multicultural, racially integrated, densely populated, mixed-income, arts-positive, progressive neighborhood on the north side of Chicago. No Exit's namesake was Jean-Paul Sartre's play *No Exit* (*Huis Clos*), which bears Sartre's most famous line, {{*L'Enfer, c'est les autres*}} ("Hell is other people"). In Sartre's atheistic vision of hell, characters with conflicting histories and personalities are condemned to stay in the same room together for all eternity and are thus robbed of their independence. Throughout high school, when things weren't good at home on the northwest side, I would often go and live with my Grampa Ed in his house in east Rogers Park and would frequently go to No Exit, as well as to another café down the street that was called Ennui, so I could drink pots of coffee, smoke cigarettes, and sulk along with all the other habitués. Suffice it to say, no-one in my high school ever voted for me to be glee-club president.

the dean's office for extreme hairstyles that I would just shave off before starting the next one. Molly dug all this about me. She started coming up and talking to me to see what made me tick. She found that I was well-spoken—books and PBS miniseries will do that to you—and that I had a lot of probing insights into the inner life due to my time spent in the trenches of dejection. Molly said she wanted to be a singer. We became buds!

And now here, all these years later, was this new boss, Anne, telling me she's good friends with Molly's family. Anne said, "I'm trying to get my daughter into that high school you and Molly went to." I decided not to mention how much I hated that high school. And I decided not to tell Anne how I never deserved to be there in the first place. As for Molly, she'd left by the second semester of sophomore year to go to a school that had a conservatory. She'd sung Sinéad O'Connor's "Black Boys on Mopeds" at the audition and was offered a partial scholarship. She said her goal was to be a voice major in college and to join an opera company right after graduation. We stayed friends for several years after she left our school, but we eventually lost touch. Now Anne was telling me that Molly had lived with her while she was studying theater, with an emphasis on voice, at her university and that in exchange for room and board, she had taken care of Anne's little girl while Anne was at work.

What a difference my first day with Anne was from my first day with the boss at the job I'd left after only one week.

ᘒ

On my second day at the for-profit hospital, I had lots of questions while learning the ropes at its law office. Anne answered a couple of my queries but then said, "Can't you figure this out? What is it? A lack of experience?" I said, "No. No, no, no. I have experience. *I have experience.* I…I'll figure it out." I went back to my desk and took a moment to drink in the music that was playing from the classical station on my clock radio.

The classical station, Classical 97 FM, never left my dial at work. I thought it'd keep me smart now that school was out. I had it on to remind me of the finer things and my aspirations to be a mature artist and to live that oh so sophisticated international-film character life. By now, with a well-trimmed and nicely parted haircut, I was spending even more time in independent film houses than I used to spend in punk clubs. It didn't make me relatable to my peer group but with a 10th house Capricorn moon and a 4th house Saturn and Mars, with Chiron on my Aires ascendant to boot, nothing ever has.

The third day, Anne asked me to get her the CEO contract that was attached to a particular case. Those were her exact words, "CEO *contract.*" I went through the files and found something called "CEO Agreement." I knew that things were excruciatingly technical in law and that it was best not to run on assumptions. So, I knocked on the door jamb of her open office door. "Anne," I said. She smiled at me, the corners of her Irish eyes lifting like the wings of a wee starling. I said, "Hi. I have this here. Is this what you're looking for? Or is this different from the CEO contract?"

I put the CEO Agreement down in front of her. She pointed to the title, "This is the CEO contract."

I said, "Oh great! Yes. I thought so. But I wasn't sure if there was some distinction between a CEO Contract and a CEO Agreement." I placed it in front of her and headed for my desk.

"Kyle," she said, stopping me at the door as she took off her reading glasses and rubbed her eyes, "Kyle, you're a smart guy, aren't you? I mean, you have a college degree, don't you? You know, my other secretaries…they had far less education than you…and they caught on a lot faster."

I stood frozen.

"But that's just an observation," she said, "You can go back to your desk."

ℒ

I didn't get any sleep that night. Instead, I laid supine in bed with wide-open eyes.

Dreading the morning to come, I remembered how James Joyce had once called Ireland "the Mother Sow who eats her children." He wasn't talking about the Celtic Tiger of the 21ˢᵗ Century. He wasn't talking about the dynamic, diverse, cosmopolitan, LGBTQIA-inclusive island that is on the vanguard of the arts, culture, technology, and democracy today—the Ireland of which I have been a proud citizen since 2007, after having filled out all the required paperwork and acquired my grandparents' baptismal records. I don't think Joyce would have recognized the Celtic Tiger or its *fin de siècle* run-up.

Joyce was talking about the Ireland of Peter Mullan's *The Magdalene Sisters*, Frank McCourt's *Angela's Ashes,* and Martin Sixsmith's *Philomena.* It was an Ireland that was gasping for breath under the trenchant heel of its British overlords and under the scourge of a relentlessly autocratic Catholic Church and school system. Not only did such an Ireland make pariahs of unwed mothers and quarry of boys who did not measure up in manliness, but account after account shows that it also lauded child abuse as next to godliness. And the abused would often grow up to become abusers themselves, generation after generation.

It's why I can no longer see plays or movies penned by Martin McDonagh. McDonagh is a modern master, to be sure, but his work hits far too close to home for me. He and I are from the same diaspora, both with roots in Galway (he on his father's side, I on my mother's). Although his parents had emigrated to London and my grandparents had emigrated to Chicago, the cultural resonance of his writing is all too familiar to me.

It reminds me of how my father used to delight in smacking me around, bringing out his belt, putting me down for sport, and making me feel as small as possible whenever he had the chance, especially when onlookers from outside the family could watch and laugh along. When I was young and unable to physically defend myself against him, I would report him to the school or to anyone I thought might help, and my mother would swoop right in with the coverup, telling anyone in charge that I was exaggerating and reminding them of how they were pillars of the community. From there, my parents would engage my siblings, all of whom were significantly older than I was, to gang up on and/or beat up on me for daring to pipe up, even though many of them had received similar treatment during their formative years—yet they were more inclined to pass this sort of treatment down and to enforce a conspiracy of silence around it than to make sure that no such violence and malice ever occurred again.

And yet these were the scions of the same father who would make sure to bring me along and use me as a shield whenever he'd go to visit his own geriatric, County Mayo-born stepmother in her little apartment in Berwyn. My father's biological mother had died shortly after giving birth to him. My Grampa Barney had to send my father, then a baby, back to Ireland until he could get his bearings and find a new wife. It wasn't until many years later, when he was an adult, that my father learned that his stepmother wasn't his birth mother. Nobody wanted to tell him this when he was growing up, lest it upset his stepmother. From what I've been told, my father's stepmother would light into him, about anything and everything, whenever she got him alone but for some reason, she would back off when her grandchildren were in sight. I'm not sure why we were such kryptonite for her, but we were. That's why he made a point of bringing us along whenever he'd go to fulfill his filial obligation to visit her. He wasn't tough enough to take this treatment from her, yet he expected us to be tough enough take it from him *and* to buffer him from her.

Grampa Barney had gone on to have two other children— my aunt and my uncle—and my father's stepmother was their birth mother. One of the more infamous stories about my father's stepmother was that, during the Great Depression, a family guest had given my aunt a doll for Christmas. My father's stepmother was not at all pleased with this. To her, the world was tough as nails, and she wasn't about to raise a prima donna. So, when the guest went home, my father's stepmother put my aunt's doll in a box and stored it well out of reach on a top shelf of the coat closet. My aunt was only allowed to play with her doll for one hour, once a year at Christmas, and then the doll would go back into the box and back up to the top shelf of the coat closet until the following year. There seemed to be no graver non-carnal sin in my father's stepmother's eyes than to spoil a child. She passed this same mentality down to my father.

A few years ago, I went to see Martin McDonagh's *The Lonesome West* at the Gaiety Theatre in Dublin. Like a thousand other Irish plays, including three or four that I'd seen on that same trip, this one is about siblings in a storm-ravaged land who are at each other's throats with tragic consequences. The actor who played the sadistic older brother was the spitting image of my late father: tall, thickset, pasty, lumbering. At the climax of the play, when it's revealed that the older brother had perpetrated an act of savage cruelty and torture on his gay younger brother's dog, I was shocked to find the theater bursting with laughter. Sure, it was nervous laughter, but I couldn't for the life of me understand how anyone could even think to laugh at something like that, especially when there was a picture of the dog, a smiling black lab, set front and center on the living-room mantelpiece on stage. I myself hung my head and wept an ungovernable flow of tears.

After the actors took their bows, the rest of the audience simply picked up their coats, bustled out of the theater, and got on with their evenings. For me, I felt like I'd had the wind knocked out of me. It was all I could do to make it to the exit door. I stumbled into Temple Bar, where I called Julius from a cobblestone alleyway, crashed my back against the brick wall of a pub, and collapsed to the ground. I broke down crying all over again. I unloaded to him about how triggering the sadism in McDonagh's play had been and how it was all too reminiscent of how time and again, I'd seen people from my own family and culture do their best to undermine each other.

To be fair, my father had never once killed an animal. In fact, one time he told me that he'd once gone on a hunting trip with some guys who'd been in the Marine Corps with him. He'd gone out into the woods with them and spotted some game. He took aim at the animal, it might have been a deer, but he couldn't bring himself to pull the trigger. He said it looked so scared and helpless, he had to let it go.

I was so relieved to hear this, but also found it wildly out of character for him. At home, he'd say, "Hello, *stupid*," with sneering, searing contempt whenever our little gray family cat Kelly would cross his path, lest he display even a glimmer of affection or vulnerability around the house. He'd give me the same look whenever he'd see me lavishing her with love and praise, which only made me propitiate Kelly all the higher. He'd point at Kelly and snarl, "That is the dumbest cat in Christendom." Whenever she would see him coming, Kelly would crouch and hide under whatever furniture was in reach.

I regret that, after I moved out of the house, I left Kelly with my parents. As she got old, she started dirtying around the house, so they put her in their workroom, left her there, and forgot about her. They literally forgot about her. They'd forget to even feed her. One day I came over for a family party and went down to see her. Kelly couldn't even stand up. She kept collapsing each time she tried. I kissed her and cried over her. I ran up to get food and to get help from my mom. My dad just stood at the top of the stairs and blustered, "What's your mother gonna about it?" For once, I knew better than to waste precious time getting into a stupid argument with him as he stonewalled with an intransigent scowl. I maneuvered my way around him and told my mom what was going on, but she was too busy playing the smiling hostess to care. One of my sisters said, "It's just a *cat*," this cat I'd raised from the time I was nine and who'd slept by my side through all those awful years that I'd spent in my family's home. But that remark didn't just slip off my sister's tongue. She knew it had teeth. That's why she said it.

My other sister flat-out rolled her eyes when she saw me crying. My dad called out to that same sister, "Hey! What do you think the longevity of the cat is?" My sister scoffed, "*Zero.*" The living room shook with laughter. It wasn't that what she'd said was at all funny or witty. It wasn't, not even a little bit. But it was flip, and it was bold, and it was nasty, and it was deflective. And they all laughed boisterously at what she'd said because it kept them all from having to feel, in a house where any amount of feeling or sensitivity was derided as weakness, if not madness.

I ran down and tried to feed Kelly. She did all she could to stretch out her tongue to touch the kibble that I held in my palm, but she was too weak to retract it into her mouth. I held her and sobbed. My brother came down and said he'd take her in to be put down. He wouldn't let me come, though. I was too much a mess. My mom did come down to say goodbye to Kelly. She gave her a single stroke. My dad just sat upstairs, laughing at the demise of the cat he couldn't wait to get rid of.

The other sister—the one who'd said, "It's just a cat"—she followed my mom into the workroom with an ear-to-ear grin and, as was her style, made herself the center of attention in our last moments with Kelly. She looked fiendishly into Kelly's half-closed eyes and reminded her of the time that Kelly had killed her pet dove after my sister, who was 22 years old at the time, had kept goading Kelly to approach the open cage, thinking she could shut it just in time to save the dove from attack. She'd done this many times before, in fact, to give the cat a start and the bird a scare and to give herself a laugh. Only, she'd done it one too many times and the cat acted on primal instinct. Now my sister was 35 and saying the words, "*So long, Kelly*," with a Freddy Krueger, horror-film drone, a Freddy Kreuger flair of the eyes, a Vincent Price laugh, and a Freddy Krueger wave goodbye as she let each of her sharp fingernails flick down, digit by digit, as my brother carried Kelly out in a carrier to be euthanized in the emergency room.

My mother plastered a smile back on to her face like nothing had ever happened and went back upstairs to rejoin the party. Everyone gathered at the dinner table, said grace, and toasted, "To the dead cat!" And they all laughed like the partygoers in *The Masque of the Red Death* did before the partygoers all got theirs in the end. And as they laughed, I got my coat, stormed out of the house, and took a cab back to my place. It was, in more ways than one, my Irish goodbye to them.

From then on, I would zealously guard any cat who'd ever toddle into my experience. I would give each cat only the most enviable life. After enough incidents like the one on Kelly's last day, I find myself unable to remember my parents with fondness; and even though I wish them all well, I know better than to let my siblings back into my life. I'm sure Martin McDonagh would be happy to have them in one of his plays, though.

A couple nights after I saw *The Lonesome West*, I met my cousin Damian for the first time. We went out to dinner at an Italian restaurant, not far from St. Stephen's Green. I told Damian about the effect that McDonagh's play had had on me in contrast to how it had seemed to affect the rest of the audience. Damian said you had to be from Ireland to understand. He had grown up on the same hardscrabble farm in County Cavan that Grampa Barney had grown up on. Until Damian could go to university in Dublin, his life had been an unending regime of punishing labor and brutal scutwork. And he acknowledged that, just as in the play, the local Catholic church loomed over their household like a wraith. He said that he wagered that a lot of the audience had either grown up in similar circumstances or that, to keep the peace, they'd learned to laugh off the meanness of people who had grown up in such circumstances. They still walked the earth after all. They were a fact of life.

But I didn't have to grow up on the Emerald Isle to know that friendly fire had long been the name of the game in my culture of origin. I had realized this decades before my dinner with Damian. And I'd realized this years before I'd even lain there watching my alarm clock flick down, digit by digit, to my next workday with

Anne. And I couldn't prove it, but I strongly suspected that by telling Anne that I was also Irish, she felt even more empowered to take up the heel up against me. She seemed to have an atavistic understanding that you were allowed to do this to your own kind. It's in the blood.

℘

I came into work the next morning and Anne shouted my name. I threw my bag down next to my chair and rushed into her office where she was thrashing through a pile of files. "Where in the hell are the files for—" and she named a whole bunch of cases. I said, "They weren't in the filing cabinet?" She said, "Don't you think I looked there? All I know is, these problems *never* used to happen with any of my other secretaries."

I decided not to respond to that charge. I simply went on a rampage, turning over anything that wasn't nailed down, in search of the files. Anne kept walking past me, shooting me death glares.

My breath caught as I said, "Anne, I swear, I never touched those files."

"And yet, right when you start working here, they go missing," she replied, "I'm going to a meeting. They'd better be here by the time I get back."

As she swung open the law office door to leave for her meeting, I said, "Anne, can I go through your desk? I don't mean to rummage through anything personal, but it's the only place I haven't looked."

"Sure," she said, "Another set of eyes. All I know is that nothing like this ever happened with any of my other secretaries." With that, she stalked out.

My hands were shaking. My heart was crashing through my chest. I went into her office. I went through all the upper drawers of her desk. I didn't see a single file.

I opened the bottom lefthand drawer.

There they were. All the files she'd named. Every last one of them, in a pile. She had taken them from the filing cabinets and instead of putting them back or leaving them on my desk so that I could return them to their rightful place, she'd stowed them in the bottom drawer of her desk and forgotten all about them.

I clutched my heart and started panting with relief. I took long, deep breaths, walked myself over to the water cooler, and began splashing water on my face to come back into balance. When Anne returned about an hour later, I gave her a broad smile and told her I'd found the files.

"Well, that's good," she said, "What's not good is that they were even missing in the first place. So where did you find them?"

I relished a pregnant pause and said, "You put them in your desk. That's where I found them."

I walked her over to the pile of files.

She flipped through the pile and saw each file present and accounted for. "Oh, well, that is a relief," she said, "*Phew*...Now... How are we going to keep this from happening again?"

My chin swung down to my clavicle. "Anne, you took the files out of the cabinets yourself and put them in your desk. That's not something I did. If you'd like, next time, you can put them on my desk after you're finished with them, and then I will put them back."

She said, "Good. So that's what we'll do." And she looked away and picked up the phone to join a conference call.

I took the files and put them back in their proper places in the filing cabinets.

♌

A round this same time, I was hanging out with my French teacher from college.

Yes, I had gone on to receive a college education despite my less than stellar high-school transcripts. But I'd only gotten into this college because I'd gotten my grades up over the course of two semesters at another local college, one which I'd hated even more than high school, but which had allowed me to redeem my academic record.

I liked the college I ended up going to, a lot. It was officially a third-tier school, but you could get a first-rate education out of it if you worked hard enough. You got out of it what you put into it, in other words. That might be true of any school, but I think it was even more true of this one. There were plenty of students who deeply digested their coursework and who did a lot of extra-curricular research so that their studies would become even more real to them. It was a mostly commuter school, where most people worked and went to school at the same time, like I did. There were many adult students, who were often single parents with full-time jobs trying to finish a belated degree. There were a lot of students who lived at home and many of those students were from immigrant families who had instilled in them an iron work ethic and a reverence for education. The college was in the same neighborhood as my old high school, but that didn't bother me like I thought it would. I hardly even noticed.

And I loved my intermediate French class.

My French teacher's name was Evelyn, and she was only a couple years older than I was. She was a T.A. working toward her master's in French Language and Literature. I couldn't help but admire her sense of style: the form-fitting leather jackets, the long wool sweaters, the stretchy pants, the dramatic foulards, and the leather boots, sometimes black, sometimes dark brown. She'd be all decked out like this at 8 a.m. The other guys in class (the class was all guys) couldn't help but admire her limpid sapphire eyes and chin-length blonde hair. It was quite a pick-me-up for them as they sipped their first coffees of the day from their paper to-go cups in class. At the time I was taking her course, I'd tell my friends that it was as though Evelyn worked in the Ivory Tower but lived in The Leopard Lounge.

Evelyn took a shine to me. Not only would I do my homework, but I'd also write up extra-credit essays with the aid of my Larousse French-English dictionary and my French grammar book. In these essays, I'd give Evelyn recaps of the French movies I'd recently rented or seen at the cinema—{{*Dans* Domicile Conjugal, *Antoine Doinel n'est plus le délinquant juvénile de* Les Quatre Cents Coups. *C'est un homme marié et un père maintenant. Il décide d'arrêter d'être un voleur et essaie de trouver un vrai travail.*}}—and plot summaries and thematic analyses of books by French authors that

I'd recently read (in translation), so I could become a more well-rounded reader and consequently a better writer.

Evelyn started inviting me out for sangria with her and her boyfriend Jim, who was also a T.A. but in Spanish. Jim was a gorgeous Chinese-American guy who had majored in philosophy in undergrad but had studied abroad in Salamanca and decided that teaching Spanish was as good a career prospect as any, which is why he was now in grad school. Evelyn and Jim were by far the most attractive couple on campus. They were probably the most attractive couple on earth. They lived together not all that far from where I was living on the north side of Chicago.

When the semester ended, I got an A in her class, and Evelyn and I started becoming friends outside of class. She even invited me to come visit her in Paris, where she was going to study at Sciences Po for two semesters while teaching English at a grade school in the 14th arrondissement. Jim was going to stay behind and continue teaching at our school.

Enfin! I could see the city where all those chain-smoking, trench-coated roués and brooding, beret-capped detectives from the movies lived! I could take those brooding walks by *la rive gauche*. I could cross the *passerelles piétonnières* above the Seine and marvel at the quick-sketch artists and poets, churning out art on demand, indifferent to the fates of their creations but intently watching the coins piling up in their hats. I could already hear the Miles Davis tracks from Louis Malle's *Elevator to the Gallows* accompanying my movements as I'd shamble down the gaslit streets of the City of Light.

I was barely making rent with my student job but with a little discipline, I managed to squirrel away enough money over the course of six or so months to buy an economy ticket to go see Evelyn over Christmas break. Jim told me he was going to go too, only he said he was going to go a couple days ahead of me. Good, I said. They'd been away from each other for three months. They needed their alone time[4].

I landed at Charles de Gaulle and took the metro to Gare du Nord, where Evelyn and Jim came and met me. I hugged them both and Evelyn said she had some wonderful French chocolate and strawberries back at the apartment. We went back to where she lived in the 13th arrondissement. The stairwell to her garret apartment was so narrow I didn't know if I could get my luggage up the spiral staircase. It took some maneuvering as we made our way up the creaking, wobbling stairs. I repeatedly jammed my suitcase into the sooty stucco walls, but we ultimately managed to get it to the main room. Evelyn said, "Here, Kyle, let me show you the kitchen." There was a staircase landing that divided the kitchen from the rest of the apartment. I followed her in, and she said here's the refrigerator and here's the sink. The room was barely

---

4   Asked why I wasn't at Christmas dinner that year, my mother told people that I was in Paris visiting my French teacher. True enough. But she couldn't just leave it there. She proceeded to tell them that I'd gone because my teacher's boyfriend was also going to be there and "Kyle wanted to make it all look proper." I had told my mother on multiple occasions that I was not a virgin and that I'm gay, yet a convenient amnesia would always set in, and she'd actively convince herself that I agreed with her position on premarital activity and that I had gone to Paris on a chaperoning mission. She also felt the need to tell others this. In her mind, a lie was not a lie if told in the service of propriety. Hyacinth Bucket had nothing on my mother.

large enough for the two of us to fit into. I wasn't sure why she was making such a production of showing it to me.

Jim said he'd already seen the kitchen enough times and he walked back down the creaky stairs and stepped outside the building for a smoke. When the front door shut behind him, Evelyn turned to me and said, "Jim's breaking up with me." Evelyn took the bowl of strawberries out of the refrigerator and started washing them with a sudden fury.

Evelyn hadn't been one month overseas before another T.A., this time one in the Spanish department, had caught Jim's eye and he'd decided he'd rather be with her. Now that the news was on the table, any graciousness that Evelyn had demonstrated between Gare du Nord and the kitchen was cast off like a burning tire necklace.

From that day forward, Evelyn was out for blood in ways that'd make Medea call the gendarmerie. A side to Evelyn that I'd never seen came out and never went back in. Every day she wouldn't let a chance to take a swipe at Jim slip. There was this *somewhat* new thing back then called email. I wasn't using it yet. Evelyn had only started using it once she got to Paris. She'd take the metro to the Centre Pompidou every afternoon, just so she could log into her email account and read the daily sweet nothings that Jim would send her from back home (cyber cafes hadn't been invented yet, let alone iPhones). Not that this was enough to stave off homesickness or lovesickness, but it helped. Now, however, on Day Two of my visit, Evelyn made both Jim and me accompany her to the Centre Pompidou so we could watch her cancel her account. He could no longer contact her, she was making clear, and she could no longer be disappointed to find that there would never again be anything from him in her inbox. Jim looked shame-faced at the floor and so did I, even though I was just an innocent bystander to all this.

We'd go out for lunch and dinner, and she would destabilize her water or wine glass just enough so it could tip but then be saved by either Jim or me. Then she'd say, "Wow. That was a close one. Wouldn't want to break the glass like Jim is breaking my heart. He's breaking up with me, you know. I just couldn't bear to see another thing around me break. Too much is breaking inside of me already." Yes, we'd gotten the point the first time she'd tipped a glass—and the second and the third time. As all three of us would be sitting together, Evelyn would make frequent and bald-faced reference to how there was a new woman in Jim's life now and to how much he was taking away from her—visits to his parents' place up the street from their apartment in Chicago, for example; walks with his parents' collies; how she'd come to regard them all, even the dogs, as family; how they all adored her; and how she would have gone to say goodbye to them in person if she'd known it was all going to be over so soon after she'd left for France.

Even though there was a new woman in Jim's life, Jim and Evelyn still slept together throughout the trip. It was all part of their weeklong farewell party, and every night I got to hear every sound of it, from the other side of the wall, as I tossed and turned on the couch. Afterwards, Evelyn would walk out and let Jim enjoy a cigarette in bed, something she'd make him take outside at any other time of day. She'd see that I was awake, and she'd curse Jim's name and rant to me about what a lousy lay he was, loud enough for him to hear every word. I stayed mum but highly doubted his performance had been the flop she said it was. I have ears after all, and all week Evelyn had been in no mood to pull a Meg-Ryan-in-the-diner scene to placate Jim. She wasn't faking it. And I could see why she already missed him.

I had wanted to take a tour of the Opera Bastille, which I'd first seen in the textbook for my History of Art & Architecture II course, but now I saw there was no need. I was already rooming with my own personal Maria Callas.

I cut my trip to Paris short by a few days and took a train all by myself to see another marvel from my art-history textbook, the Uffizi in Florence. I had invited Evelyn to come along with me but only because I knew that she couldn't. She had kept talking about what a tight budget she was on. I was on a tight budget too, but I also sensed I couldn't afford to stay in her place one more night, even though she wasn't charging me a single franc to sleep on the couch. So, instead, I stayed for two nights in a $15-a-night hostel in Florence and hung out with a couple American students I'd met in line at Brunelleschi's Dome. They were both studying in Bologna. We toured the museums and sat around cafes talking about how Europe had broadened them in ways they didn't yet have the words to describe. From there, I arrived back in Paris the night before my flight back to Chicago and stayed at a backpacker's hostel. I did not visit Evelyn one last time nor did I tell her that I was in town. I simply caught my flight back the next morning.

I've looked it up and scholars have confirmed that there has never been a worse first visit to Paris in history, with the possible exceptions of a few military campaigns. The trip to Florence was another huge bite out of my budget, money I would soon need for rent, yet it all seemed worth it. My heart went out to Evelyn for her suffering, but not for the suffering she felt it was her right to dole out to me, as collateral damage for being in the same room as Jim.

So why was I hanging out with Evelyn now that she was back in Chicago?

Well, I'd recently gotten dumped by a bi-curious guy named John. Mostly all John did when I first met him was neg me about being gay—nothing I hadn't experienced before, just unoriginal micro-aggressions: mocking my gay voice (something I've never been able to do anything about); slackening his wrist when talking to me; slipping in the words queer and queen; however, he was post-punk and wearing a tight black leather skirt and red stockings at the time, which he reasoned exempted him from any charges of homophobia. We had friends in common, though, including his roommate Alex, so I thought I had to put up with him. That's how it is when you're 22. You let your peers get away with shit, lest you end up with no friends. Better to be sorry than lonely, even though you're bound up to end up all the lonelier and sorrier.

The thing that saved John from the social ostracism he so richly deserved was that he was devilishly attractive: willowy, Teutonic, with a square, steel jaw and azure eyes. Works every time. He could diss anyone in the most hurtful ways and still be invited back for the next party because he'd been so unfairly blessed with a comely aspect.

And then when I was between apartments, I ended up crashing on his couch because, again, he was roommates with my friend Alex who said I could stay with him. And then John and I started hanging out. He began to win my sympathy as he'd express to me all the hurt he'd endured in his early alcoholic home. He liked that I had such an attentive ear and such a comforting shoulder to cry on as he and I would sit on his and Alex's couch, which had become my makeshift bed. And then one thing led to another...and then I started sleeping with John in his bed. Once he even said, "I love you, Kyle." That sent me reeling for about a week. It was Number One with a bullet on the best-moments-of-my-life charts. Until he recanted. He said he'd said it, but he didn't mean it. Not even as a friend, he qualified. "It doesn't come that easy to me," he said. And then John told me he'd decided he only liked chicks. And then I told him he'd led me on, that he'd treated me like a toy he could toss into the trash once he was done with it. And then he smirked, and then he laughed at me.

And then I moved out and vowed never to speak to him again. And then the friends we had in common, including Alex, sided with him and dumped me. He got invited to the best parties, after all. I could only offer free, unlicensed therapy sessions and deep-dive explorations of the soul over cold espresso drinks and dirty café ashtrays. And then my best friend at the time, who hated John and had admitted many times to having a mad crush on me, even though she was engaged to another guy (and what part of "I'm gay" was she not getting?) decided to dump me as a friend for going out with John in the first place. And there went just about my entire social life.

So, I was lonely and that's why I didn't hang up on Evelyn when she'd called me the summer after I graduated from college. She knew someone I knew, and she'd asked him for my new number and he'd given it to her. She'd sent me a few letters after I'd come back from visiting her in Paris, but I never wrote back to her, given the shitty time she'd shown me after I'd spent all the little savings I'd had to go see her. But I had a plausible and innocuous excuse when it came time to offer her one: I'd had to move out of my old place after they'd raised my rent and then I'd had to couch-surf for most of my last semester in school. Now I was living in a rundown apartment in south-side gangland. So, at the time she'd sent me her letters, I didn't have time for anything but completing my final papers and exams, going to work, and keeping my arms out of a straitjacket. That was a suitable enough answer for her, so we made a date to meet up at a tony little bistro in Gold Coast called 3rd Coast, where I could only afford to order a coffee.

I was the first to arrive. Once the hostess had led me to a table, I heard someone behind me call out my name. It was Evelyn, rushing up to me from the doorway with arms outstretched. She was a lot rounder than she had been when I'd last seen her. In fact, she hadn't been round at all then. Now, though, I found myself instinctively backing up a pace or two as I hugged her. I thought she might be expecting, and I didn't want to harm the baby. I didn't say anything about it, but she could tell that this was what I was thinking, given how careful I was being. She said with a wave of a hand, "No, I'm not, don't worry. I just…let myself go."

We sat down. I ordered a coffee, and she ordered a glass of Bordeaux. That's when she explained that after Jim left her, she'd started overeating and had also started drinking red wine by the jug. The drinking still hadn't taken its toll on her face, though. She said that for the last half of her stay in Paris, she had started going off with random men she'd meet at bars or even on the street. Once she thought she'd caught something horrible from one of them, but her test came back negative. It turned out to be a simple bladder infection, but it was a wake-up call nonetheless. So, she said she stopped going off with guys and decided not to look for love until she got back to Chicago. She also said she'd joined a gym and planned to shed the excess weight post-haste.

I've always been a sucker for people's self-improvement plans. I thought the simple act of signing up for a gym membership might be the first stage of metamorphosis for Evelyn. That hope vanished as quickly as it came over the course of our conversation.

After slagging Jim off for a good half hour, she finally asked me how I was doing. I'd told her things hadn't been going well for me either, but that I still had a few weeks of free counseling and medical care left at the university, even though I'd already graduated. I said I was taking advantage of it while I still could. I revealed to her that I'd gone on Prozac because I was hurting so much in the wake of how things had ended with John and my erstwhile best friend, as well as all the erstwhile friends who'd gone with them. Evelyn took a slug of wine, put her hand on mine, and said, "Oh, gawd! You poor thing. You know, I mean, I get depressed a lot, but if I had to go on medication, just shoot me now!"

I'd seen her at her worst in Paris and didn't want her freaking out on me by freaking out on her, so I just smiled and let it slide.

She turned back to the subject of how much she missed Jim, even though she still hated him. I asked if they'd had any contact. She said she'd called him once from Paris, but he'd simply stayed mute on the other end of the line. Finally, she'd said, "Don't just sit there breathing. Be a man! Tell me you don't want to talk to me anymore." And Jim decided to "be a man" and told Evelyn that he didn't want to talk to her anymore. And so Evelyn said, "Fine. Fuck you," and hung up. That only felt good for an hour or so, though. She proceeded to drop all the graduate courses she was taking at Sciences Po that semester and only went through the motions when teaching at the grade school. The rest of the time, she floundered around, drinking and hooking up with strange men. She conceded, "No matter who or what I do, the grief hasn't gone away." She huffed, put her hand to her heart, and bowed.

"Well, why not take a page out of the WASP handbook for this one," I said, hoping to inspire a new resolve, "Turn back to the lost art of keeping up appearances. In the meantime, let the grief pass when it passes." This was my polite way of telling Evelyn it's unattractive to go around ranting and raving everywhere you go. I told her about an essay I'd read on Jackie O. I'd never had any interest in the Kennedys before, but I'd found the essay so inspiring in the wake of what had happened with me and John and all the friends I used to have. True, Jackie wasn't WASP, she was Catholic, but she was still high society and set a high premium on comportment. The essay talked about how Jackie led a life of grace and poise and decorum, rarely if ever complaining, in the aftermath of the assassination. I told her that, after reading it, I'd even stand at bus or El stops in the same posture in which Jackie

had stood when her husband's coffin passed for the last time. I had
a lot of heartache too, I said, but I'd resolved to handle it stoically.

Evelyn flipped me off.

I smiled like it was a joke. It wasn't and I knew it wasn't.
Yet I played it off like everything was copasetic between us and
continued smiling until she shot me a look of rage, at which
point I reverted to taking a sip of coffee, which hid my smile.
Her hostility faded away soon after and the night ended on a
pleasanter note.

And the next day, I got the call telling me that I'd gotten
my first job out of college, with the humanitarian organization.
I had a fatter paycheck on the horizon so I could move out of
my south-side hellhole and into a cozy studio in the lovely, leafy
Ravenswood neighborhood on the northside before starting my
new job. Things were looking up.

And then I walked out on that first job after a week and had
to temp for Anne.

Meanwhile, Evelyn's job teaching French at the university
was right there waiting for her now that she was back. What I
wouldn't have given to be back in the Shangri-La of school. Those
days were over for me, though, but they weren't for Evelyn. She
got to teach two classes in something she was good at, and she
got to be the boss of her classroom. No, she wasn't raking it in as
an adjunct, but she did get tuition waivers, she had no student
loans left to pay off, and a plum part-time job had also landed in
her lap. A French woman she'd become friends with through the
French department owned a business where she leased apartments
to Americans traveling to Paris. She had asked Evelyn to come

work for her two days a week. She said she could really use her help, especially since Evelyn spoke fluent French. She offered her an incredibly generous salary. Evelyn got to practice French every day at both her jobs and, at her friend's workplace, she was given an office with a sleek desk, floor-to-ceiling windows, and a killer view of downtown Chicago. The hours were flexible, there was no enervating downtime, and the Frenchwoman was hardly ever in the office at the same time as Evelyn. She had ample autonomy and extra cash. And yet all Evelyn could do was complain about how she had to work two jobs and how she was single.

And even the latter misfortune was starting to clear up. Word had started going around among friends of her friends that she was back in town and unattached. And where my phone never rang with offers, guy after guy was calling her and asking her out on dates. With each subsequent meetup I had with her, though, her rages about anything even mildly imperfect got worse and worse, and I wondered how long it would be before guys would take note and stop throwing themselves at her feet?

❧

Well, not as soon as I'd secretly hoped they would…
Because by the time I got back to my apartment on Missing Files Day at Anne's office, I saw there was a message on my answering machine. It was from Evelyn. She said: "*Kyyyyle!* I'm in *loooove!*"

Evelyn said in her message that the night before, she'd gone out for Beaujolais Nouveau with a friend from work. She said they'd met these two guys who were in town from Paris. "One of the guys is named Lucien," Evelyn said, "And let's just say... he just left my apartment. He stayed the night, and he says he wants to see me again. And get this: he travels all over the world making documentary films! I mean, are the gods smiling on me or what? I'm going to have to, I don't know, become a candy striper or something to *earn* this good karma...I mean, he's gorgeous and he...Oh, and his colleague's name is François. And guess what, François is gay! But I don't know if you'd be into him, Kyle. I mean, he's *oooold*. He's probably like, 37!—And did I mention that I'm in *looove*?"I called her back. She said, "Do you want to party with the French boys tonight?"

After the week I'd had at work—and there were still a couple more days to go in it—I needed something to take the edge off. And it wasn't good for me to be alone in an apartment where there were sharp knives beckoning me from the kitchen. So, I said I'd go.

It was a cold October evening. I took the El down and met her on the Belmont El platform. We stood in a blustery, wintry wind and bundled into our coats. There had been reports on the news that El riders had petitioned City Hall to turn on the heat lamps on the El platforms. The signers must have been a bunch no-names, though, because the city refused to honor their request. They said it was too early in the year, even if it was unseasonably cold, and that everybody had better suck it up and bundle up or else freeze to death.

Evelyn decided she'd get our blood pumping by telling me all about how Lucien was the best lover she'd ever had. "Twice the man Jim is," she snarked. Lucien knew just how to handle a woman, she said. Going by Evelyn's account of their first night together, it was clear that Lucien had been all around the world in more ways than one. Their combined repertoire, which Evelyn spared no detail in annotating, was enough to make the *Kama Sutra* look like *Reader's Digest*.

Adding to Lucien's laundry list of attributes, she said that he was so secure in his masculinity that he had no problem with his colleague François being gay. They were even sharing a hotel room and he didn't feel the least bit threatened by François's sexual orientation and he wasn't the least bit concerned about whether people in the hotel would think they're lovers.

Evelyn had also been seeing another guy, someone we both knew, the guy who'd given her my phone number. That guy's name was Bob. He had also been a student in the French class where I'd first met Evelyn, but he was about 10 years older than I was. At the time, he was thinking of going back to school for a second bachelor's degree, maybe in psychology, maybe in biology, with an eye toward med school. He wasn't sure. And two years later, Bob was still working as the head waiter at a French restaurant in Bucktown and still casting around for what he might do next with his life. He had gone to Paris and had gotten together with Evelyn right after I'd left. In Paris, Evelyn had told me she'd agreed to have lunch with Bob but that she wasn't looking forward to it. Bob swiftly became one of the men she had tried to get over Jim with, though, as soon as they'd wound up back at her pad in the 13th arrondissement. Now that she was back in Chicago, however,

Evelyn kept complaining that it wasn't working with Bob. He just wasn't doing it for her.

And now that Evelyn had experienced Lucien, Evelyn was more than ready to give Bob the boot. "I mean, the battle of the names alone," she said, spreading out her hands with a marquee-headliner flourish. "LUCIEN," she said with full European aplomb and "BOB," she said with a flat Midwest accent and a shrug. She let her hands fall, *splat*, at her sides upon mentioning Bob's name, as though she'd just let a pancake that she wasn't even planning on eating fall to the ground for some other poor shmuck to pick up and take to the trash. She said that Lucien and Bob were both 33 years old but whereas Bob was waiting tables and still finding himself, Lucien was an international man of mystery, blazing a trail in international documentary filmmaking. She said, "I feel like calling Bob and saying, 'I met a guy named *Lucien*. He's the same age as you. He's a French film director who is paid to document world cultures. You're a waiter, who thinks just going out to eat at Indian or Turkish restaurants and commenting on the food is enough to make you cultured.'" She laughed at how Bob paled in comparison.

I said, "Evelyn, please. Just…don't go after Bob's job title, okay? I mean, I get that you're not excited about Bob, but please, don't slam him for being a waiter. I feel so much more like Bob than that Lucien guy these days. I'd hate to think people are saying those kinds of things about me."

Evelyn asked why I was being so sensitive all the sudden. I tried to suppress my tears, but they burst out of my eyes. I told Evelyn about Anne's "You have a college degree, don't you?" comment and about the files she'd stowed in her desk before blaming me for their disappearance. Evelyn put her hand on my arm and said, "Oh my God! Your boyfriend dumps you, your best friend dumps you, the rest of your friends dump you, you had to quit your first job out of college because of an abusive boss, and now you move on to *another* abusive boss? Things just keep getting worse and worse for you!"

Now that she'd summed up my life for me like this, I considered throwing myself on the third rail and sizzling on it in the freezing cold. Instead, I stepped on to the El when it showed up.

When we reached our stop, we walked over to Lucien's boutique hotel just off Grand Avenue and waited outside. Lucien came out of the building with his colleague. Lucien was everything that Evelyn had sung about and more—a swarthy, exotic dreamboat with the easy smile and *je ne sais quoi* of the accomplished. And there stood François. He didn't look old at all. (At 49, as I type this, I'm the first to protest that 37 isn't old!) I'm six foot two, and he was only a few inches shorter than me. Cropped black hair, copper skin, deep chestnut eyes. He was also wearing black leather pants and a tight-clinging black leather jacket with a zipper at the left breast pocket and a tight green neckerchief tucked into the collar. All my time sitting alone through matinees in film centers had served me well. I knew a Fassbinder fantasy man when I saw one, and this one was French like Querelle[5].

5   In Rainer Werner Fassbinder's last (and unfortunately worst) film, *Querelle*, the title character is Belgian, not French. However, Fassbinder based his movie on Jean Genet's novel *Querelle de Brest* (1947), where the title character is from the Brittany region of France; so, Querelle's fictional provenance is France, not Belgium.

I could forget all about Anne for one night.

ℐ

"*Enchanté*" François said as he leaned in to shake my hand. It turns out they do say that in France. I was too busy refereeing a post-breakup to notice when I'd gone there the first time.

Lucien asked where we should all go to dinner. I said I knew a place. I used to work in the neighborhood and knew of a bistro just around the corner called Harry's Velvet Room. Showing off how I wasn't your average Midwest hayseed, I mentioned how Harry's had all the noir atmosphere of the places Inspector Maigret would swagger into when he was hot on the trail of a suspect. Lucien and François caught the reference and laughed with recognition. I considered it an early triumph.

This was way back when people could smoke in bars and boy, did they ever smoke at Harry's, especially cigars. You could see their ever-billowing wisps curling against the low-lit red lights and scarlet, crushed velour curtains. For added ambience, there was a quote from Freud, framed above the bar: "Sometimes a Cigar is Just a Cigar." François checked the open menu that was encased in glass on the outside window. He saw they served artichokes, his *légume préféré*. We decided to give it a try.

The hostess told us she could have a table ready for us in half an hour if we'd like to wait at the bar. So that's what we did.

Lucien was putting the moves on Evelyn. She leaned into his half-embraces but also gave him the what-for: "Look, I hope you're not thinking that I'm one of those girls…You know what I'm saying, 'a girl in every port.' I've been through the wars, *mon pote*. People break up with me and leave me to pick up the pieces." Well, it wasn't really "people." It was that one guy, Jim, her old boyfriend. She'd also had a husband when she was 21, but she'd been homeschooled by her evangelical parents when she was growing up and had rarely gotten to leave their dismal little west suburban apartment except to go to church. She'd met her husband in college, and he was the first person she'd ever slept with. She hadn't been his first, though. She didn't find that fair. So, after they tied the knot, she started having affairs to make up for lost time. He found out about it and filed for divorce. So, I guess the divorce was a breakup, but it wasn't without cause. Still, when flirting with Lucien, she counted it as proof that she'd been hard done by.

I started speaking to François…in French. I marshaled everything I'd learned in Evelyn's class and in the couple other French classes I'd taken after that. His eyebrows were raised in pleasant surprise at how I was rolling along. Except that I kept addressing him with the formal *vous*. Eventually François stopped me and said there's a more casual pronoun, *tu*, which you can use when speaking to your peers. I knew that, but I was having a hard time thinking of this European filmmaker as my peer. I was an office temp and wannabe author. But he seemed to prefer to be regarded on the same level as me, so I confirmed: <<*Puis-je vous tutoyer?*>> And he said, <<*Ouais*>> like it went without saying. So, I babbled on in French, this time using the familiar *tu*.

When speaking any language, even English, I tend to be as flamboyant as Tina Turner often was by the bridge of a song. I make grand, bravura gestures even if I'm just describing, say, a new salad they've started serving at the corner diner. When walking down the street telling one of my stories to a friend, I've even caused hard-sell street preachers to put down their bullhorns, mid-jeremiad, and lean in like, "Gimme a second, I gotta hear this." What can I say, I've mastered the art of making mountains out of molehills.

Contrast this to François, who stood with a polite smile, so out of keeping with the French stereotype. He would frequently interject, *Oh là là* (yes, it turns out they say that too) as I carried on about my contact with French culture via language classes, art, film, and a pen pal that I'd had for years but whom I had lost touch with. "He lives in Claremont-Ferrand," I said in French, "Or he used to. It's been so long since I've heard from him. We used to write to each other all the time. He says that Claremont-Ferrand isn't much of a town. I always pictured it being the Fort Wayne, Indiana of France. But he was too busy to notice how boring it was since he was in law school there. He was always studying—I mean, you know, he'd take breaks. He used to write to me a lot, for example. He's never been to Paris. At least not when I knew him. Can you believe that? Well, maybe he's been there since, I don't know. If I'd been able to find him, I would have asked him to come visit me in Paris when I went to see her," and I motioned over to Evelyn who was now smooching away with Lucien.

François said, << *Oh là là.*>> (I think he was saying this in response to me. I could tell he was avoiding looking at what Lucien and Evelyn were up to. So was I.)

I continued (in French), "Listen, I would LOVE to have a French pen pal again. Can I write to you?"

He said, {{*Oui. Tout à fait.*}}

Back then I always had my book bag with me, a black messenger bag that went with all my clothes. I carried it around so that I could have a book with me wherever I'd go. Whenever I had a free moment, I would read so I could grow smarter, not dumber, in the absence of school. The real world, in the form of Anne and the boss from my first job, was making it abundantly clear that I was a total disappointment and ignoramus. That's how teachers used to treat me too before I learned how to bowl them over with big words and purple prose. Now those teachers weren't there anymore, aside from the one who was making out with Lucien a few feet behind me, and I assure you, my ability to turn a phrase was the last thing on her mind at that moment in Harry's Velvet Room. Whatever cut the mustard in the Ivory Tower, I was learning, wasn't worth a mustard seed in the real world. And it was becoming clearer by the day that I didn't have the stuff—the inborn competence—to make it in said world. I would have to play to my strengths and bone up on books so I could pull off a dark-horse victory as a writer. Hence the book or two I always had in the messenger bag, which I was reaching into now so I could find a pen.

I found a blue Bic pen and handed it to François. He wrote down his address and telephone number on a napkin. He said, "Maybe you can visit me in Paris."

I said, "I'd love to. I'll have to save money first."

He said, "You're welcome to stay *chez moi*. If I'm in town. I'm often out of town, out of the country, on assignment."

I said, "And you can visit me any time if you're ever in Chicago again." I wrote down my address and phone number on another cocktail napkin and handed it to him. He said *merci*, folded the napkin in half, and stuffed it into the back pocket of his leather trousers. Meanwhile, I put the cocktail napkin he'd given me, with his phone number and address on it, in between the pages of a hefty book that I was reading and which I'd dug out of my bag, *Hopscotch* by Julio Cortázar. I said, "The author is Argentinian, but the story opens in Paris. It's about a young Argentinian writer, who's kind of the author's alter ego. He's trying to start his author career in Paris. Have you read it?"

François said he knew the book. He'd read parts of it, not the whole thing.

"Where are you going after Chicago?" I asked him.

He said, "L.A. and then San Diego. And then Mexico. And then I'll be in Africa for three months. We have a lot of filming to do."

"*Oh là là,*" I said, remembering the old Sassoon Jeans commercial, "That's...incredible."

And all I kept thinking was, How does anybody get a job like that? And more importantly, how does anybody command the level of respect to get promoted into a job like that?

But I didn't say that to him. Not right away anyway. I simply stuck with technicalities, "So you're not going home at all?"

He said, "No. It's just a time where we have a lot of projects all at once."

And I stood there considering my job, which I already hated but was clinging to like a life raft, lest I get fired from it and wrack up yet another massive failure in life. And I thought, "Projects! Why can't I get a job that has 'PROJECTS'?" I just answered phones and made coffee and put files back in their right places after Anne would yell at me for misplacing them, even though she was the one who'd misplaced them. I was constantly applying for other jobs, but I wasn't getting interviews, even though the counselors at the graduate center had reviewed my résumé and had said it looked polished and professional, especially for a recent grad. Still, I couldn't find a permanent job, much less one where I could show that I could write. Other people my age, who were good at numbers or graphic design, were already getting gigs in accountancy, finance, ad design, or this new thing called website building. They could demonstrate their talents, and soon enough they were taking on PROJECTS. I was constantly searching the want ads and going back to the job center to see if there was something out there that involved writing. But I couldn't find anything. And so, I wondered if it was my Sisyphean task to keep working for the Annes of the world until they'd just decide to fire me. And yet here I was, talking to a French filmmaker who was booked all year, all around the world, with Projects.

And then François asked me, "What do you do for work?"

I said, "Well, I'm a writer but I have to work another kind of job to support myself, so I work for a lawyer." I wasn't writing anything of merit yet, but that was my goal, so I felt secure in proclaiming myself a writer.

He said, "Oh, okay," and nodded.

I was happy to see that he was willing to let it go at that. I really didn't want to talk about my day job. Not that there's anything wrong with being a legal secretary. I've worked with enough of them to know that they're some of the best, most competent, most indispensable people on earth. It's just that I obviously wasn't scoring high as one myself and was desperate to become a François instead, albeit in something writing-related, preferably in *creative* writing. It had to make you feel good about yourself to have the kind of high-profile, high-powered job he had.

I said, "I wish I could travel around the world, especially for work. I wish I could find a profession like that. Not in film. I'm no good at technical stuff. I don't even know how to use the Internet[6]. I keep trying to find a job where I can write but I just can't find one. And other people my age are finding jobs in things they're good at." And then I offered a seeming non sequitur: "You know who Mick Jagger is, right?"

François said, "*Oui*, of course, I like Mick Jagger very much."

I said, "Oh, me too! He's my hero. He's so sexy. So smart. And he works the stage like nobody else. And he didn't want to be a singer. He wanted to make a lot of money as a banker. He was going to the London School of Economics. But he loved the blues. And one day, he walked to the train station in Kent, holding a stack of

---

6   Most people didn't at the time.

blues albums that had been imported from Chess Records, right here in Chicago. And Keith Richards just happened to be crossing his path. They had known each other briefly, in childhood, and Keith Richards recognized him and said, 'Oh, 'ey, man. 'ow's it goin'?—Where'd you get those records?'⁷ And they started talking. And Keith told Mick there was this guy named Brian Jones, who was starting a blues band with him, and he said to Mick, maybe

---

7   How Mick Jagger had become my hero: By around age 17, I went back to basics and started delving deeply into the discographies of The Beatles, The Rolling Stones, The Velvet Underground, David Bowie, Bob Dylan, and other mainstays that had influenced the more contemporary bands that I was listening to. Jagger especially became a figure of fixation for me. Not only was the Stones' 1962-1972 oeuvre, with a couple exceptions, either genius or near-genius, but I came to regard Jagger as the androgynous equal to David Bowie. (I no longer hold this opinion. Bowie's genderfluidity was far more committed, creative, conceptual, and complex.) As Alan Bloom said of Jagger in *The Closing of the American Mind*, "He was homosexual, he was heterosexual." There was even a pervasive rumor, fomented by David Bowie's ex-wife Angela Barnett, that Bowie and Jagger had been lovers and that Jagger had written the song "Angie," not for Angela, but for *David* Bowie. According to Barnett, it was an affair that Mick feared would end both their careers if it were ever exposed, hence the alleged reason that Jagger sang, "Ain't it time we said goodbye?" In college, I wrote a pretentious term paper for my Post-World War II British Literature class in which I compared Nicolas Roeg's 1970 film *Performance*, which stars Mick Jagger as a reclusive rock star, to Ingmar Bergman's crypto-lesbian 1966 film *Persona*. In *Performance*, Anita Pallenberg, who plays one of Jagger's live-in girlfriends (she was Keith Richards's real-life girlfriend at the time), calls Jagger's character "a male-female man." As a young gay man, I took great solace in the fact that there was an artful and confident archetype like Jagger that I could look to as I navigated the straight world with frenetic unease. I used to do lip flexes and even lip push-ups against the back of my hand so I could plump my lips up to look like his and I would lip-synch to Stones album after Stones album, hour after hour, in front of my bathroom mirror as a means of invoking the spirit of the still extant Jagger. By the time I met François, I had deliberately dropped rock and picked up classical, which I thought would help me focus on launching a writing career. I was still a rabid fan of the Stones' best work, however, even though I wasn't actively listening to it. François, as it turned out, only knew a few of their hits and regarded them more as a stadium act and classic-rock relic.

there's a place for you in it. He didn't know if Mick could play guitar or bass or drums or if he could sing a lick, but he could tell by their conversation that Mick knew the blues, so Mick went to meet Brian Jones, and Brian Jones made him the singer. And that's how it all got started. Mick was 18."

François said, "How old are you?"

I said, "23."

His eyes went wide, "Oh, you're *youuunnng.*"

"Oh, I don't know about that," I said, "I'm five years older than Mick was."

He said, "*Oui, mais,* you don't want to be a rock star."

"Well, I do," I said, "Just not with music."

I think I lost him there. He looked at me screwy. But he just took a sip of his Cabernet (I had one too) and said, "You're young. You're still in the domain of the possible."

"What were you doing when you were 23?"

"*Oh là là.* Let me see, I was new to Paris. I was working for a radio station. I was writing reports and press releases…"

I thought, oh, I wish I could get a job at a radio station writing reports and press releases. Writing *anything* other than phone messages.

Yet I'd harped on my hard luck enough for one night. Until I was due back in the hoosegow of Anne's office, I wanted to bask in the glow of this adept, who seemed to move with such savoir-faire in a realm where nobody ever diminished him, where he didn't know what it was to be belittled and trampled underfoot. Or, at least, I couldn't imagine he did. Not as he appeared to me right now.

So, I changed the subject, "How long are you in Chicago?"

"We leave tomorrow morning."

"Oh, do you like it?"

He said, "Yeah, I like Chicago."

"Is it your first time here?"

"*Oui.* I've always wanted to come here."

"Really?" I said, "Why?"

"When I was *un petit garçon,* growing up in Lyon, I saw a postcard of Chicago and it had these groups of skyscrapers and I said, '*Oh là là!* I have to go to Chicago!'"

"Yeah, we do have those. Do you like skyscrapers?"

"*Oui*, I like skyscrapers very much."

"Have you been to New York?"

"*Oui*," he said, "I've been to New York many times."

"I've never been there."

"Really? Never?"

"No," I said, "I sound like my old pen pal, don't I? He'd lived in France all his life and had never been to Paris. I guess that's me with New York. I've just lived here my whole life."

Lucien tapped me on the shoulder and told us our table was ready.

François ordered the artichokes and something else, I can't remember what. *À table*, I dropped the names of a lot of French authors, artists, and auteurs, the filmmaker kind of *auteurs*, that is. François and Lucien could see I'd done my homework, and speaking of homework, Evelyn told the table that she used to love reading the assignments and extra-credit work I used to turn in for her class. "They read like film reviews," she said, "And book reviews too." François mentioned a lot of old Hollywood films that he loved—*Gilda, Heaven Can Wait, Giant, Sweet Bird of Youth,* and more—and he talked about how they often play them in the cinemas of Paris. I had just happened to see most of the movies he'd mentioned. At some point in college, I had bought Leonard Maltin's book of movie reviews and tried to watch all the three-and-a-half and four-star movies listed in it. I thought it'd help me with my writing. As I talked film, I was able to show François that I wasn't the pudden-head that Anne thought I was.

François then said that *Night of the Hunter* was his favorite movie. That's the one where Robert Mitchum plays the conman preacher who has LOVE tattooed on the fingers of one hand and HATE tattooed on the fingers of the other. I said I hope he knows that not all Americans are like that. François smiled and said, "Well, obviously, *you* are not."

At one point in the conversation, Lucien said, "There's this new drug. You can get it at the pharmacy, at least you can in Paris. Have you heard of it? It's called Melatonin. It's supposed to make you sleep better and look better and, and, and, and *feeeel* better."

I said, "Yes, I know. I take it to help me sleep."

Lucien said, "Ah! *D'Accord!* Do you see, François? If you take Melatonin, you can look like Kyle."

François stared into my eyes and said, "Well, then, I'll buy a whole box."

ℒ

A fter we settled the bill and left Harry's Velvet Room, Lucien
said he'd like to go to a bar. He added, "We can go to a gay
bar." I said I didn't know of any around their hotel, except for a
really lame one for gay suits. Lucien said François had rented a car
and could drive us to another one. I suggested one in Boystown
called Roscoe's. Everyone said they were up for it. I knew I had
work at Anne's office in the morning, but I didn't want the night
to end. The rental car would turn into a pumpkin soon enough
and dreariness and humiliation would go back to being the order
of my day. Yet for at least another hour, I was spending the evening
with two French filmmakers.

We drove to Roscoe's. I wasn't a regular there. I wasn't a regular
at any bar. Occasionally, I would force myself to leave my apartment
and go to one. I'd order a beer. I'd rarely finish it. Sometimes my
eyes would lock with another guy's but I'd get nervous and look
away, all while affecting the composure of some 1960s French
film star like Jean-Paul Belmondo. I'd soon find myself back in
the safety of my apartment, reading a two-ton George Eliot novel
or doing other esoteric things, like watching yet another film I'd
rented from Facets Multimedia, never admitting to myself that I
actually found Ingmar Bergman really, really boring, as evidenced
by the fact that I always fell asleep halfway through his movies.
The more time I spent alone, though, the more rarefied my tastes
became and the more unrelatable and undatable I became, and
there seemed to be no way of stopping the cycle.

And this was in the days when I had the kind of looks that got looks. Those days are over. People still say I'm handsome, but I haven't noticed guys stargazing at me, and I live more or less in Greenwich Village now, where guys stargaze at other guys all the time. So why didn't I make hay while the sun was still shining? Why wasn't I setting up shop in Boystown and booking five dates a week?

Well, part of it was that I'm an introvert. We can only take people in small doses. Part of it was also that I couldn't relate to a lot of gay culture. I wasn't into dance music, and I couldn't stand the cattiness and superficiality of so many of the gay men I'd met. What I wanted were deep conversations. Good luck finding those on the club scene.

And lastly, there was good ole Catholic guilt. It's something that a lot of LGBTQ+ people in Chicago, which has the largest archdiocese in the world, were (and probably still are) also struggling with. But too many dealt with it by getting wasted so they could forget their inhibitions and let loose. Call me a goody two shoes (and part of me is a goody two shoes, not everybody's shadow side is a serial killer), but I didn't want to end up with the addiction monkey on my back. I had enough problems already, so I'd stay in and read most nights.

Yet here I was at Roscoe's after midnight with my former French teacher and two French filmmakers. The club had mostly emptied out, save for a handful of stragglers. A few groups of guys were dancing on the neon dance floor to some pumped-up, high-octane diva house music. A couple guys were going at it with each other in the dark corridor that led to the dance floor. It occurred to me that I might never have a night like this again, so I threw my usual frugality out the window and asked François if he wanted a beer. He said yes, so I ordered us two Sam Adamses, paid for them, and then we clinked pints and said, "*Santé!*" Evelyn and Lucien were flirting and cavorting about six feet away from us.

François asked me if I was from the city originally. I said I was. He asked if I grew up near the bar, which is in one of the more happening neighborhoods. I said, no, I grew up on the other side of town, in what is probably the least happening neighborhood. He asked if my parents know I'm gay. I said, yes, they know. I said I'd told them many, many times over the years, but they were bigots and moralists. They didn't approve, and they didn't like people who are different. And yet, I told him, I still hadn't cut them out of my life. He nodded. He understood.

François asked me if I go to this bar often. I said no. I'd been there every now and then over the past few years, even before I had ID, but not all that often. He asked me if I go to parks. By the way he said *parks*, I assumed he meant cruising parks where you hook up with strangers. I'd seen Fassbinder. I knew the things he used to get up to in the Tiergarten. I said no.

"Heart of Glass" started playing on the video screen. I sang along. I told François I like Debbie Harry. He didn't respond.

François took a sip of his beer. He said, "I'm old now. I don't know if I could pick anyone up here." I said, 37 isn't old. I told him I had a sibling who was older than he was. He smiled. He let his gaze linger. He kissed me. It was a long, passionate, two-tongue kiss and he knew just how to do it. Nobody had kissed me in five months, and those were ones that John did on the sly. This was

unabashed. And he was French. And this wasn't a movie. This was
real. I was no longer living vicariously, through the use of subtitles.

He looked deeply into my eyes and said, "You're beautiful."

I didn't respond. I simply took a seat on the barstool behind
me. He took a seat on the one next to mine and held my hand.

"You've never been to New York?" he said.

"Never" I said.

"Well, perhaps I could meet you there someday" he said.

The bar was closing. François had only drunk half a beer, so
he was fine to drive. Lucien asked him to take him and Evelyn
back to her place. François said he would, and he said he'd take
me back to mine. We dropped Lucien and Evelyn off in front
of Evelyn's building in Edgewater and I told Lucien that it was
nice meeting him and to have a safe flight and he said it was nice
meeting me.

François drove me to my apartment. After he parked in front
of my building, we shared a long, drawn-out goodnight kiss in the
car. He wanted to come upstairs, but I told him I had to get up
early for work. Everything had happened so fast; I didn't know if I
could handle it going any faster. I said good night and "I hope we
meet again." And he nodded. The rental car sped off and rounded
the corner on Montrose Avenue.

I went upstairs to my apartment, got into my jammies,
laid down on my bed, and stared at the ceiling until my alarm
clock went off. Then I got ready for work and took the El to
Anne's office.

It was a gray day. There was a note on my desk full of things Anne wanted me to do. The note also said she'd be out at a conference all day. I breathed a sigh of relief.

I opened my book bag and took out Cortázar. I flipped to the pages that held the napkin. It was still there. The ink on it hadn't blurred. François's address—which he'd said, in passing at the dinner table, was right above Cimetière du Montparnasse, where Sartre and Simone de Beauvoir and Edith Piaf are buried—was still legible and intact.

I looked at the clock. François and Lucien had probably left the hotel by now. They'd be in California soon and then they'd be off to Mexico and then Africa, with no stopovers in Paris. It'd be three months before François would be anywhere near his apartment. There'd be no contacting him. I kicked myself for not inviting him up.

I walked into the file room to put some files back in the cabinets. There was a little barred window over the southernmost cabinet. The sky was gunmetal and cloudy but there was no rain in the forecast. This wouldn't be a romcom ending. There would be no grounding François's flight so he could come running back to me in the downpour. I put the files back where they belonged, locked up the cabinets, and gazed through the bars at the sky, where François's plane would soon be.

I reached for a song, any song that could give me a good cry. I thought back to {{*Devant Le Garage*}}[8], which Nino

---

8   The English title is, "I Will Wait for You," composed by Michel Legrand and Jacques Demy.

Castelnuovo and a young Catherine Deneuve sing[9] to each other in *The Umbrellas of Cherbourg*[10]. It's in the sequence that occurs the night before Guy the auto-mechanic (Castelnuovo) goes off to fight in the Algerian War. The star-crossed lovers float along a moving sidewalk and croon their undying love for each other. They go up to Guy's room and consummate—would that I had with François—and that's how Geneviève (Deneuve) ends up with a croissant in the *grille-pain*; only by the time she finds out, Guy is off fighting in remote climes, perhaps never to return. It would have been the perfect song for this occasion, but I didn't know the words, even though the year before I'd sat through the movie three times in a single weekend at the Music Box Theater, just so I could watch this scene and hear the song over and over again.

As I stared at the deepening gray in the sky, the only other song that came to mind was Lena Horne's "Stormy Weather," and the only reason I knew its refrain was because, when I was a kid, it was on a commercial for an old-standards collection that had a 1-800 number attached to it. They'd also played "Stormy Weather" that past Sunday morning on Classical 97's *Metro Golden Memories Hour*, so it was still fresh in my mind. It didn't make sense to sing it now, though. There was no storm brewing outside. On the other hand, there was no sun up in the sky either. So, I sang the refrain anyway, and it did the trick. The rain fell from my eyes in the file room.

---

9   Well, neither Castelnuovo nor Deneuve actually sang this or any of the other songs in the movie. Since they weren't trained singers, they just lipsynched to the voices of professional singers that Jacques Demy had dubbed in.

10   *Les Parpluies de Cherbourg*, 1964, director Jacques Demy.

Thank God Anne wasn't in to see me like this.

ℒ

One thing I haven't mentioned yet is that I wasn't working full-time for Anne. She could only give me 20 to 25 hours a week. It made me feel like a loser. Wasn't I at a point in my life where I should have been working full-time and overtime, like important people do? And yet here I was working part-time at a job I couldn't brag about like others my age could brag about their jobs. This was in the days when rents were more affordable, but I was still only just getting by on what I was making with Anne. So, I would try to get in as many extra hours as I could each day before Anne would come in and say an annoyed, "Go *hooome*, Kyle." I was pinching pennies, but then again, I didn't go out a lot, so my biggest expenses were books (mostly used) and video rentals, so I managed to stay in the black.

And where I had once had a French pen pal in Claremont-Ferrand, who'd never even been to Paris, Evelyn had a pen pal in London, who'd been absolutely everywhere. By this I mean, at any given time, her London pen pal had ten boyfriends and at least twice as many guys on the side—at least according to Evelyn. She'd said he worked for an escort service and that his job description went beyond being mere arm candy at gala balls. Evelyn had started comparing my empty dance card to how her pen pal's name and number were scratched into the toilet stalls of every gay bar in London. Moreover, since he was so transient, one would see constant scratch-outs where his old numbers used to be, as well as a new update for his new number, provided by who-knows-who. And this showed that her pen pal had friends where I had books. I got to constantly hear about how her pen pal was fearless where I was a coward. He was taking on a new romance every day, and I was safely longing for a Frenchman whom I hadn't invited up and who'd driven away in a rental car. Would Evelyn's pen pal have let that happen?

And one day after work, I went to Evelyn's office downtown, at her French friend's apartment rental service for Americans in Paris. Her French friend (her boss) was out of the office and Evelyn just so happened to be on the phone with her pen pal from London.

They had started corresponding as teenagers, back when Evelyn was still a nice evangelical girl. He'd kept news of his proclivities quiet until shortly after they'd both turned 21. That's when Evelyn started confiding in him about things she'd been doing behind her then-husband's back. And that's when her pen pal came clean about the things he did for a living and the things he did for fun (those things being, more or less, one and the same). Soon they were giggling and comparing notes on how far they had each gone with their exploits, and how far they might go next. It became a game of double dare. Ultimately, she was served divorce papers, and he was diagnosed with HIV.

Now, however, she was telling me that he was deep into a regular, paid gig he'd gotten as an on-the-town journalist for London's gay scene. Subscriptions were supposedly pouring into the premier alternative rag that he was writing for on account of his column alone. A mainstream outlet wanted to syndicate it and a producer had approached her pen pal to make a biopic of his daredevil life. So now, in addition to being the real-deal gay man, he got to be the in-demand writer. Not me, the one who'd told myself I was channeling all my sexual energy into creativity and that *that* was the secret to success as an artist. No, he was the real artist, the one who was spreading his sexual energy to every Tom, Dick, and Harry and reaping a career harvest from it.

And when Evelyn told him that I had just swung by her office, her pen pal asked why I wasn't at work. And that's when Evelyn dealt the *coup de grâce* by telling him, this bon vivant for whom I was a mere foil, "Kyle only works part-time."

This was nothing I wanted the world to know.

I was always on the hunt for a new gig. As the months ground on, Anne was as much the termagant as ever. Day after day was more of the same: blaming me for things that she'd misplaced or that hadn't been done because she'd forgotten to tell me to do them, and then not apologizing, nor becoming more gun-shy.

"I don't have to take this," I started manning up and telling her as I'd stand up and push back my rolling chair, once with a storming Wagnerian orchestra from Classical 97 backing me up, "I'm doing my job. I come in early, I stay late. I leave nothing undone that you've told me to do. And all I get from you are insults and accusations." And she'd turn on her heel, head into her office, and lock the door. I would sit at my desk and try to regulate my breathing. And I would keep my ear fastened to Classical 97 FM as I invoked a grandeur that transcended this administrative oblivion. I kept expecting a call from the agency telling me that Anne had called and wanted me replaced. But the call never came.

❧

Once when Anne was in one of her better moods, she came in and told me that she had been to a party at the McGrory's house over the weekend and that Molly McGrory had been there. "She looked great," Anne said, "The best I've ever seen her."

I didn't pursue this part of the conversation further. I didn't want to ask Anne if she'd mentioned to Molly that I was working for her. I was sure that she had said something about it, and knowing Anne, she had also sighed and told Molly what a lost cause she'd found me to be. I was sure that Molly had wondered what had become of me in our time apart. I'd certainly wondered about Molly. We'd been pretty tight at one of the most vulnerable and pivotal times of our lives. And I'd hoped that she would think that by now I was about to blow up as a writer. But now the word was on the street: I'd only ended up as an underperforming lackey in her old boss's office.

How had Anne treated Molly, I'd been wondering, when she worked for her? Molly was also Irish, which probably made her as fair game for Anne as I was. But Molly was also the daughter of a friend, and it'd most likely been a friendship that Anne had wanted to keep, so maybe she'd gone a little easier on Molly. Who knows.

In any event, Molly now knew what became of me. But she did not know that I knew François.

And I clung to the napkin that had François's address on it. And I wrote the address down on another piece of paper that I'd taped to the inside of the top drawer of my desk at home so that

I would never lose it, even if I were to lose the napkin and/or the
Cortázar book.

François occupied my mind all day and night. He'd probably
forgotten all about me, though, as he plugged away at all his
projects and picked up other guys. Nonetheless, the more I let his
image settle into my brain, the more I felt like it'd taken me up a
notch or two in life to have made his acquaintance.

It'd gotten to the point where, if Anne or anybody else would
ever talk down to me or make a dig at me, I'd think, "Don't you
know who I am? I know François." He was a breed apart from all
of them, and always would be. And now I felt like I was too, by
association. If only Molly McGrory could have heard about this
instead of whatever failing performance review Anne must have
surely given me and conveyed to Molly.

On the day that Anne told me that she'd been to that party
at Molly McGrory's parents' house, I'd been opening all the
correspondence that had come in from over the weekend. Anne
sat down on the chair on the other side of my desk. It was one
of the only times we'd actually "hung out" in the office. I had
Classical 97 on, of course. Maurice Ravel's *Boléro* was playing.
Anne lifted her arms and pretended to click castanets. She said,
"Do you remember that terrible movie?" I said, "With Bo Derek?"
She said, "Yeah-esss. I think they gave it an X rating." I said,
"Leonard Maltin thought it was one of the worst films ever made."
Citing Leonard Maltin was a way for me to let Anne know that
I knew my books, film, and art—and I hoped that my playing
Classical 97 FM would help her to see this too. These aren't things
your average dumbfuck does, now are they, Anne?

I asked how the rest of her weekend had gone, other than the party. Anne said she and her daughter's godmother had taken her daughter out to dinner for her birthday. She unzipped her purse and produced a picture of her newly 13-year-old daughter, the one Molly McGrory had once been an au pair for. It was a profile shot. The daughter's eyes were open wide, and her mouth was dropped in astonishment. She was cradling a small black velvet box in her hand. I asked what was in it. Anne smiled and said, "Diamond earrings." She said her daughter had complained to her that she was too controlling and demanding. Anne said, "I know. And I have to work on that. It's just, left to her own devices, she won't push herself." The diamond earrings were a sort of peace offering she'd made to her daughter, and she said she also hoped they would make the other girls at her daughter's school look up to her.

Anne told me that now that her daughter was a teen, she could tell her things that she used to keep secret from her. Now she could tell her that she and her daughter's father had divorced because he was a skirt-chaser and wasn't doing enough to succeed at work. She could tell her that nobody had less to do with the money she used to find under her pillow or the painted hard-boiled eggs and jellybeans she'd find in a basket full of synthetic grass by the fireplace or the presents that she'd find so expertly gift-wrapped under the Christmas tree than the Tooth Fairy, the Easter Bunny, Santa Claus, or her father.

Anne told me she was relieved to finally be able to get real about the birds and the bees with her daughter too. She said that behind their townhouse in Lincoln Park, there was a carriage house that they'd rented out to some college girls. One Sunday morning, when her daughter was in third grade, she and her daughter were having breakfast with the kitchen windows open. They heard all this groaning, as if someone was in pain. The daughter became worried. Anne got on the phone and called the carriage house to see what the trouble was. I said, "Oh no," knowing where this story was going. Anne cringed and laughed and nodded, "Her roommate said, 'Oh, it's nothing. She's just…Her boyfriend's over. I'll knock on the wall and tell them to keep it down.'" Her daughter had come up to the phone wringing her hands, wanting to know what was happening. Anne thought fast and told her daughter that one of the college students (they were all business majors) was just rehearsing a monologue for an audition. I said, "Yeah, for the lead in *Bolero*." We both doubled over laughing.

It would be the last of the two or three lighthearted moments Anne and I would ever share.

Anne got up, creased down her vest, and said, "Enough fun and games."

She walked back into her office and got back to business.

If the conversation had gone on longer, I might have told her about my new boyfriend. I'd often see her in the main hallway, chewing the fat with the Operations Manager, who wore a rainbow-flag bracelet and who would camp it up in front of one and all, mentioning his partner every few seconds, just to show how out and proud he was. He and Anne would even go out to lunch together from time to time. If he could mention his partner to her, I surmised, then maybe I could mention my boyfriend.

In my head, I'd already started calling François my boyfriend, even though a wiser part of me knew that he'd left me behind in the exhaust of his rented pumpkin carriage and the contrail of his flight to LAX.

I hadn't invited him up. I'd left him with so little to remember me by, except that I'd seen his favorite movie, *Night of the Hunter*... but big deal. Lots of people had seen it. *The Simpsons* had even parodied it. In the "Cape Feare"[11] episode of the fifth season, Sideshow Bob has "LUV" and "HAT" tattooed on the three non-thumb fingers[12] of either hand as he pumps iron in the prison rec hall to avenge himself on Bart.

How far did I think that was going to get me with François?

ℰ

For however delusional I may have been about François being my new boyfriend, it was still as obvious to me as to anyone else that I had a long, long way to go before I could reach François's Olympian heights.

First things first, I needed a new job. And why didn't I just quit working for Anne and make a full-time job out of looking for a new job? Well, money was an issue, for one thing. I didn't want to have to move in with my folks. Also, I'd already walked out of one job without having anything else lined up. To walk out of two seemed like a testament to total personal dysfunction.

---

11   [sic]

12   Three being the maximum number of non-thumb fingers allowed for characters in most cartoon series.

Plus, I had a mother, one who used to call me almost every day. And unlike my siblings, I've never been any good at lying, which meant that as my mother would pry, I'd tell her exactly what was going on, no matter how much it might disappoint or fluster her, instead of telling her what she wanted to hear, something my siblings were past masters at. If I were to walk out on Anne with no other job to fall back on, it would eventually come up in conversation. And my mother would cry with the squall of a banshee and tell me that she's going to start yet another novena for me. I couldn't face that conversation, so Anne it would have to be, for now.

Apropos of novenas: Folded into a royal purple cloth, right next to Cortázar or whatever other book I'd happened to be reading at the time, I kept a rosary hidden in my messenger bag. I used to keep a Ryder-Waite tarot deck in that cloth, but I'd chucked it into a dumpster one day because I'm prone to panic attacks and it was always giving me the worst cards. Now I had a rosary stored in its place. I wouldn't have had it there if I hadn't been at the end of my rope.

The only person I had left to hang out with was my former French teacher, whose life was so much better than mine but who could never stop complaining about it. My name, address, and telephone number had been on a napkin that François had folded up and stuffed into the back pocket of his black leather trousers. By now, the napkin was probably singed to ashes at whatever Los Angeles dry cleaner François had happened to take those Lederhosen to. Such was the desperate situation I was in. I did not believe Jesus was God, but I had to admit that some Force was God, I could just feel it. And I felt I needed to make contact with that Force, and Catholic prayers were the only ones I knew at the time.

So after work, I started taking the El downtown and slipping into St. Peter's Church at Madison and Dearborn. I would sit in a pew and say a rosary or two or three there every day. I had several family members who worked within a few blocks of the church, so it was always a stealth mission for me, slipping in. I didn't want any of them catching me. I had a heretic's reputation to uphold after all.

I went to St. Peter's asking God for a new job. And I was asking for a life where I could shine like François. Back then, I wasn't using the term "inner peace," but I was asking for something like that too—for emotional stability, and for friends I could be close to and who would stand by me. I would light candles in front of statues of the Virgin and the replica that St. Peter's had of Michelangelo's *Madonna della Pietà* on the eastern wall, and I'd simply say, "Please, please help me. I'm not sleeping right. I'm feeling hopeless all the time. I'm lonely. Please help me."

Now, don't get me wrong. I didn't make any promises that I would return to the Catholic faith, and I didn't attend Mass. I'm gay and they've been horrible to us, as well as to women and to children and indigenous peoples. But I had said prayers before in my life and I'd found peace and help in doing so. And so, again, that's what I was doing at St. Peter's: saying the prayers I knew.

I've since learned that this is not uncommon either:

I know a woman from Colombia, who was raised by a widowed mom who was very devout. This woman lives with her partner of two decades, a man she is not married to. She stopped attending Mass after she left her mother's home to move to the United States and she has since been appalled, enraged, and disgusted by the Church's abuses. And yet every so often, she will pop into St. Patrick's Cathedral in Manhattan either before work or on her lunch hour, and she will dip the fingertips of her right hand into holy water and cross herself and look up at the Cross hanging above the altar and say, "God, I just want you to know I'm here. I'm with you. And I hope you're with me too." Then she'll cross herself again and leave.

I've known actors here in New York who are lapsed or ex-Catholics like myself, and who even say they're atheists, but they have confessed to me that on the horns of an important audition or in the pits of despair over missing out on a part that was all but guaranteed them, they have been known to sneak into St. Malachy's, the actor's church on West 49th Street, to pray for help—even if all they could hope for is the strength to keep going, or for a sign to do something else with their lives.

In San Francisco, I had conversations with fellow dharma practitioners who were also raised Catholic and who had also left the Church, but they also told me that they still stop into churches when they're open so that they can light candles and sit in pews to find peace. They even admit to saying the prayers they knew as children while they're there.

None of this means that we've rejoined or "come back" in the way the Church uses the term. It doesn't mean we buy the theology. It means that we have touched into something we knew growing up that brought us a sense of comfort, security, and even miracles. And having grown up in a pluralistic society, and having watched enough *Oprah*, I've come to believe what many others believe: That there are many paths to the Divine and that God will accept prayers from all traditions and from non-traditions. And, also, that temples, churches, *sanghas*, mosques are all powerful centers for prayer and meditation where we can feel the energy of all the prayers that have ever been said in those domains and that this can bring enormous consolation, hope, and empowerment.

And so that was more or less where I was coming from when I'd go to St. Peter's.

And I'd always see this downhearted African-American woman who'd sit on a turned-over milk crate outside, begging for money. Working for Anne, I didn't have a lot left over after rent and bills, but I always gave something to this woman. I'd wrap larger bills into smaller bills so it wouldn't look like I was giving her that much at first and then I would slip them into her paper cup and skitter away, hoping not to be noticed, although sometimes I'd hear her call out, "Thank you!" My heart has always gone out to homeless people and by then I'd even started volunteering to serve them breakfast on Saturday mornings at a nondenominational soup kitchen in Uptown. But now I felt the threat of destitution all the more powerfully, even though there was no rational basis for it as I had a lot of family—family I didn't get along with, but family still—in the area who would have considered it their duty to scrape me up off the streets if it ever came to that. My anxiety said otherwise, though. We never know what combination of factors has put someone on that milk crate, and now I was having

my own experiences of instability and I'd hoped to God that my
fortunes would go up, not down.

After going to the church, I would board the El again and before
going all the way home, I'd stop at the Borders bookstore at
Diversey Avenue and Clark Street. Now that I was already at the
point where I was saying rosaries in a church, I wasn't too hip to hit
the self-help aisle too. Help was something I was clearly in need of.
I had once fancied myself too cool to even look at Julia Cameron's
The Artist's Way: A Spiritual Path to Higher Creativity, which I used
to see in just about every bookshop window in town. Contempt
prior to investigation: I'd written it off as bourgeois piffle that no
real artist would buy. And now I was the one bringing the book
to the cash register. And I brought it into the cafe area after I'd
paid for it and began to read it. The book talked about bringing
God into our creative pursuits and how we did not have to follow
organized religion to have a deep and abiding relationship with
God. I was so glad somebody said it. I kept reading.

Cameron explained the process behind the Morning Pages,
where you do three pages of longhand, stream-of-consciousness
writing every morning. She talked about what a difference the
pages had made in people's lives and art, especially when paired
with "artist dates," where you go on your own to do something
that interests you—to a movie, a restaurant, a museum, a park, an
arts-and-crafts store—and she counseled us to watch as new ideas
and synchronicities would sprout for our... *projects*. Yes, now I
had a project. And she was making clear that our foremost project
in life is our own life. As Chekhov himself said (and I didn't know

he'd said this until I'd read *The Artist's Way*): "If you want to work on your art, work on your life." Julia Cameron said you can be as petty and crabby and self-pitying and obnoxious as you want to be in the Morning Pages, and they don't even have to be well-written. All that matters is that you write them. Furthermore, you weren't supposed to show your pages to anyone. She said that they are simply a conversation between you and whatever your concept of God is.

I thought to myself, a conversation between me and God where I can be as bitchy and petty as I want to be? With that, I was on my way to Walgreens to buy a new notebook for my first round of Morning Pages, and for the first time in a long time, perhaps for the first time ever, I wanted to wake up in the morning. And the next morning, I did just that. I'd set my alarm clock for an hour earlier than usual and I woke right up and started my first round of Morning Pages with the words "Dear God." 26 years later, I still start them with those exact same words every morning.

The Artist's Way became my Bible. I read it obsessively and did all the exercises in it religiously. It was extremely well-written, crammed with wisdom, and Julia Cameron had a vast and varied life and career that I could have only dreamed of having. And I saw that Julia Cameron had quotes from many poets, authors, and spiritual teachers that I had never heard of: Meister Eckhart, Theodore Roethke, Thich Nhat Hahn, Swami Saradevananda, and Natalie Goldberg, whose writing methodology I'd soon be taking up. I started migrating over to the spirituality aisle and reading about eastern philosophy. I started reading self-help books by the crate, books that I would have considered woefully anti-intellectual not one year before. Now it's true that some self-help books are better than others, but what I appreciated most about the genre was that the good self-help books were written in a simple, user-friendly style that was so much more digestible than the hoary, impenetrable tomes we had to read in college and unlike those tomes, these books offered hope, something nihilistic authors used to tell me I should be strong and stoic enough not to need.

I also started to carry in my messenger bag a copy of Jon Kabat-Zinn's *Wherever You Go, There You Are*. Wherever I went, there it was. Upon Kabat-Zinn's advice, I started folding my pillow in half, sitting cross-legged on it, and meditating, according to Kabat-Zinn's instructions, for half an hour every morning after doing my Morning Pages.

I could feel a new life opening up, even though I was still in a thrall to Anne.

I did go to the career section too, to see if there was a book that could tell me how to get the hell out of Dodge and maybe teach English abroad, but I had a sibling who had spent a couple years abroad as part of an international volunteer mission after he'd had a hard time finding a job. He got to see the world but then came back and holed up in my parents' basement for the better part of a decade. The world was simply too vast and complicated and overpowering. It wasn't until he was in his mid-thirties that my folks finally kicked him out. I wasn't going to set myself up for a basement-boy life. I decided to stay put and face up to my struggle on the home front.

Unless of course François would call and beg me to move overseas to be with him, and then maybe I'd consider it. Yet I was still sane enough to see what a fantasy this was.

♋︎

A couple French expressions would help here. *La douleur exquise* ("the exquisite pain") is the feeling of longing for someone who is missing or otherwise entirely unattainable. It hurts and distracts like the worst crush you ever had in high school, but it also has that chic, wistful element of adult yearning. There's a certain pleasure in the pain of having this missing person always on your mind.

Martin once told me about a fellow yogi he was training with in India. Her teacher had died. Every morning, she would light candles in the shrine room and sit gazing with tender affection at his picture. Martin said to her, "You must really miss him." With awe and bewilderment, she said, "Yes. Isn't it wonderful." That's *la douleur exquise* in action.

And although he hadn't died or left me a picture or even a scintilla of spiritual wisdom, this was pretty much how I felt about François. Life was wherever he was, and he was gone.

There's another French expression that exquisitely describes the desideratum of *la douleur exquise*: *Il brille dans son absence* ("He shines in his absence"). The memory of François lit up every corner of my mind, as did the mirage of him.

He wouldn't be in Paris for months. That's what he'd told me the night before he left Chicago. The napkin with his name and address on it rested unmolested between two pages in *Hopscotch*, as did the back-up paper taped to the inside of the top drawer of my desk. What sat atop this same desk was the Larousse French-English dictionary and the French grammar book that I had once used to write extra-credit essays for Evelyn's class. Now I decided to use them for help in crafting letters to François, so that I could let him know that he was not forgotten, and so that I could make sure that I would never be forgotten.

Yes, before all this, I'd told myself that I'd wanted to spend my nights writing the Great American Novel. Only I had no ideas for one, not even with the help of the Morning Pages. So, instead, I whiled away the evening hours penning letters to François in French. It was hard work. I had to look up every other word. But it was a lot of fun too. It was a sort of highly focused scavenger hunt for words and idioms. No doubt, I was using many of them wrong or out of context. But that's all a part of language arts, isn't it?

Plus, I'd read that after Sartre had been conscripted into the army, he and Beauvoir would write to each other for something like seven hours a day. (Sartre didn't see much combat during World War II. Although he was fiercely committed to the resistance, while in active service, he mostly sat in a bunker and smoked and wrote letters.) This is what intellectuals do, isn't it? This is also what people who are in love do, I thought. And I had Classical 97 playing in the background as I wrote to François, to remind myself of the realm beyond the workaday, beyond Anne. Yes, I'd play the same radio station in her office, but somehow the music took on a whole different tincture in my apartment, even if the DJ was spinning the exact same symphonies.

And I started writing to François about my humdrum life. I couldn't afford good stationary, so I simply bought stacks of loose-leaf paper and boxes of Mead envelopes from the school supplies aisle at the corner drug store. I didn't even leave the margins blank as I rolled my pen along the thin blue lines. I wrote about how much I resented Anne. How she would find any excuse to upbraid me so that she didn't have to face her own personality defects, her own lack of organizational skills, and her own failures—her failed marriage being just one of them. In these letters, I'd turn the tables on Anne. Now I was the one giving *her* a failing performance review. I'd write to François about how disconsolate the jaundiced walls and mousy brown carpeting and achromatic filing cabinets were in the for-profit hospital's law office, and I'd contemplate what was wrong with a society that would even have such a thing as a for-profit hospital.

But I'd also write about how crisp the air is in the fall in Chicago, and I'd write about the beauty of the setting sun that I'd see flaming out over the courtyard apartment buildings on my evening walks through the neighborhood. I told him how the cold was setting in, but how this also gave me a chance to wear my favorite gray thrift store overcoat, a dark red Shetland wool scarf, and a Greek fisherman's hat. I'd walk to Lincoln Square, where one could find beer halls and buildings with Bavarian façades. I told him how, between my getup and the locale, I felt like I was well on my way to becoming a saturnine European author in my own hometown. {{*Parfois, il faut regarder le rôle avant de pouvoir y grandir.*}}[13] I said I knew how pretentious that might sound, {{*mais*

---

13   "Sometimes, you have to look the part before you can grow into it."

sans nos prétentions, nous ne serions jamais devenus trop grands pour nos casiers.}}[14]

I'd write reviews of all the films I was renting or going to see at the Music Box Theater, Facets Multimedia, the Three Penny Theater, and the Fine Arts Theater. I refrained from mentioning the mounds of self-help books I was poring over—I didn't want him to think I was a head case—but I would describe in detail the novels I was reading, or had read, or the plays I'd go see whenever I could get a cheap ticket. I saw James Goldman's *The Lion in Winter* at the Raven Theater, for example. I'd already seen the 1968 movie starring Katharine Hepburn, Peter O'Toole, and a young Anthony Hopkins. The play at the storefront theater didn't have the budget or star power of the three-time Academy Award-winning blockbuster, of course, but I told François that this did not stop me from feeling the pathos of Eleanor of Aquitaine as she is furloughed from imprisonment in England, all so that she could journey on a barge to her estranged husband's chateau in Touraine. {{*L'isolement cellulaire a dû être une torture*}} I remarked, {{*Mais au moins elle a pu aller en France pour Noël.*}}[15]

I told François how inspiring it was for me to know someone like him, someone who goes to so many countries and sees so many cultures and studies their ways. I told him that I thought Proust was only correct to a point when he said, "The real voyage of discovery consists not in seeking new landscapes, but in having new eyes." I told him that although I had read four volumes of *In*

---

14   "but without our pretentions, we'd never grow beyond our pigeonholes."

15   "Solitary confinement had to be torture, but at least she got to go to France for Christmas."

Search of Lost Time, I'd first seen the pull-quote on a poster that had a picture of a sunflower field on it. It hung in a coworker's cubicle at the civil-service job I used to have when I was still a student. This was the same coworker who had taped the back of an empty NutraSweet packet to the base of her computer monitor. The packet bore the apocryphal Confucian proverb: "He who rows the boat rarely has time to rock it." I said I thought that by coming up with this poster quote, Proust was rationalizing his decision to live as a bedbound agoraphobe in a cork-lined room, and I said that I thought that by having it pinned to her cubicle wall, my coworker was just being sour grapes since she herself wasn't able to go anywhere, other than to the office, on account of the bedbound mother she had at home; and, as for the NutraSweet packet, it was clear that she was reminding herself to keep her head down lest she lose the only source of income that was keeping her and her mother in house and home. *{{Telles sont les vies des personnages kafakïens}}*

And speaking of Kafka and the transformative power of travel, I relayed to François, in the best French I could, an apocryphal story that Kafka's lover Dora Diamant told about him after his death. Supposedly Kafka had been sauntering in a park in Berlin, where he saw a little girl crying inconsolably because she'd lost her doll. Together, they looked high and low for the doll but came up emptyhanded in their search. Kafka told the little girl to meet him in the park the next day and he said they'd take another look around. The next day he presented the little girl with a letter that he said had been written by her doll. It said: "Please don't cry. I am not lost. I have gone on a trip around the world. I will write you letters about my adventures!" Kafka and the little girl agreed to meet up in the park every so often and each time, he would read to her another letter that the doll had written from one exotic location or other. The doll's worldview was expanding by leaps and bounds every time she met a new person in a new land and the little girl began to look forward to the doll's letters with as much anticipation as she used to look forward to her playtime with the doll when it was still living with her at home.

After many such meetings, Kafka met up with the little girl one last time and told her that her doll was back in Berlin! And he just so happened to have her with him. The little girl jumped up and down, clapping her hands. Kafka asked the little girl to close her eyes and hold out her hands. The little girl complied, and Kafka placed a doll into her palms. The little girl opened her eyes but shook her head in confusion. "This doesn't look like my doll at all," the little girl said. And that's when Kafka read the little girl the doll's final letter in which she explained, "I'm not like I was when you last saw me. My travels have changed me." The little girl hugged her doll and took it home.

Kafka died a year later. I told François that the cynical side of me finds it creepy that a forty-year-old man was having these meetups with a little girl. {{*Et où étaient ses parents, ou sa nounou?*}} Yet, I told him, the less cynical part of myself wanted to see the beauty and innocence in this story. And I said that this more trusting part of myself believed that if this was the last thing, or even if it had been the only thing, that Franz Kafka had ever done in his brief life, then he deserved an eternal paradise, the likes of which his stories and novels suggest he'd never seen in his time on earth.

And the story of the doll didn't even end there. According to Dora Diamant, years later, the little girl, who was now a young woman, found a note tucked into the doll's outfit. It was from Kafka. It read: "Everything you love will likely be lost, but in the end, love will return to you in a different way."

I told François that I hoped this story would find him well when he returns from Africa, and I asked François how he feels his travels have changed him. I told him I was dying to know.

I asked him, {{*Puis-je t'écrire tous les jours?* }} That's French for, "Can I write you every day?"

It was a rhetorical question. I didn't even wait to hear a response. I was too much in the flow of writing to him.

In other letters, I'd describe how I was thinking I could go back to school for something. *Anything.* Except creative writing, I said. MFA programs are so snooty, I told him, and people tear your work apart in workshops because (a) they're competitive and (b) they can't just give compliments, that's not what's called being honest. The whole thing was too discouraging to even consider attempting. I said maybe I could go back and take a bunch of non-degree courses, like Bob had, except maybe I could take them all in art history so that I could get into a grad program for it and become an art historian who studies, and is surrounded by, art all day long. I imagined it must elevate one's spirits to immerse oneself in the study of beautiful creations. It also seemed to me that being an art historian is kind of like being an artist, except you don't get kicked around in dead-end day jobs all day like artists do, like I did at the for-profit hospital.

But to go back to school for post-bac classes, I would have to beg money from my parents, and I didn't want to do that. First, I wasn't sure they'd give me any, even though it was a Clinton stock market and my dad had made more money in it than he'd ever made working that slip-and-fall lawyer job he'd had all those years. But if he did give it to me, it'd come with strings attached. He'd tell me I'd have to go to Mass and seriously consider becoming a Catholic again, and that wasn't going to happen. So, I wouldn't be going back to school for quite a while, it looked like, even though I missed it. It was in undergrad, after all, that I had professors describing me by a word that had never[16] been used to describe me before or after: *smart*.

I didn't mention my volunteer work at the soup kitchen, that was too goody-goody, but I did tell François about how I had started volunteering at some nonprofit performing-arts companies, thinking it might lead to a job. What it ended up leading to was me walking down State Street in a giant red lizard costume amid a team of dancing skeletons while a bunch of grade schoolers from the Chicago public school system sucker-punched me in the back. And then there was that oh so artsy theater in Pilsen that I was taking tickets and doing clean-up for. They were doing a series called *Sex Fest: 69 Plays in 69 Days*. Each play was more lurid than the next. They would take place in an inflatable pool full of sex toys, for example, or in front of a projection screen that had

---

16   It is true that Anne had said, "Kyle, you're a smart guy, aren't you?" but that was a setup for a smackdown, so it doesn't count.

kaleidoscopic patterns of porno sequences playing on continuous loop. Each play was performed by actors who were working day jobs that didn't sound one bit better than the one I had with Anne. And once, before we were able to begin setting up for yet another *Sex Fest* show, I saw a performance art troupe, who was renting the space for a few hours, rehearse a piece in which they were doing a eurythmic dance in black leotards while singing the dirge: "*Learn to accept limitation and failure forever.*" This was *so* not the philosophy of *The Artist's Way* and I wrote to François: *{{Oh, s'il te plaît, dis-moi qu'il y a plus dans la vie que ça après la fac.*[17]*}}* I wrote to François about all these things.

I did not, however, tell him that I'd go to church and say rosaries for a new job and new friends before working the ticket counter for *Sex Fest: 69 Plays in 69 Days.* I was afraid he wouldn't write back if I did.

ℒ

B ack then, it took two 29 cent stamps to send a letter by regular mail to France. I splurged on a few rolls. And every morning before work, and on weekends, I would drop another letter to François in the USPS mailbox on my way to the El.

Playing it cool was not my strong suit at 23.

By the time François came back to Paris, the concierge of his building told him he had a couple boxes waiting for him. There were over 90 letters from me in them.

---

17   "Oh, please, tell me there's more to life than this after college!"

ℒ

Evelyn had asked me to meet her for a drink one night on Clark Street. "Ya know," Evelyn said, throwing back a cognac, "Lucien called. He told me about the boxes and boxes of letters you sent François."

I said, "Was François freaked out?"

Evelyn said, "He was *surprised...Buuut...*François told Lucien they were well-written."

I said, "I thought filmmakers get letters like that all the time."

"Not without calling the cops," she said, "But don't worry. I covered for you. I told Lucien to tell François that Kyle's a writer. He writes to everybody that way. Which was a lie, of course. I mean, I wrote you letters from France—after a breakup, no less!—and I never heard squat from you. But now François is walking off with these volumes, penned in the very blood of your heart. What's up with that?"

I wanted to say, "Well, first off: you're not a hot French guy. And secondly, you showed me the worst of times when I should have been having the best of times in Paris," but I knew that I'd be dead meat if I'd dare to be so candid. So, instead, I said nothing.

And she went on and kvetched about her department. She said she'd been written up at work. She'd been walking down the hallway to her office at the same time as Jim, so she gave him the finger. Jim reported her. The head of the department launched an investigation. There had been witnesses, one of them being Jim's new girlfriend, the Spanish T.A., but a couple neutral parties had also corroborated Jim's record of events. Within no time, Evelyn was proven guilty. "It creates a hostile work environment," the chair of the French department told her, "And we don't allow that here." Evelyn said it wasn't fair, but she promised to keep her middle finger to herself next time.

And then Evelyn casually dropped the bomb on me. She told me that she couldn't go to Paris with me the following year. Our plan had been to save up and go together. That way, she could see Lucien and I could see François. Now she was telling me she wouldn't be able to get the money together. I didn't understand this lack of money she was always talking about. She was single and childless like I was. She was making more money than I did, working at jobs she was actually good at. She had the same bills I had and no loans to pay off; the school had waived her tuition since she was teaching. Her rent was less than mine, and yet I'd still found a way to put $40 a paycheck into savings, which was steadily building toward the purchase of an economy ticket.

I thought she'd crushed my dreams with this news. I had thought it'd make me look less desperate if I were to go with her to France. That way, François would be more inclined to think I wasn't going there just to see him, that this was all part of a larger trip we'd planned. And then it occurred to me: Hadn't I made myself look desperate enough already with my preponderance of letters? Maybe I wouldn't need to use Evelyn as a diversion. That thought cheered me up. I began to relax.

Next, Evelyn started moaning about her parents. She had gone to their apartment that past Sunday. Evelyn's mother had also been a French teacher. She'd taught at the local public high school, which was one of the highest-ranking public schools in the country, but she wouldn't let Evelyn attend it because there was no God in the public school system. So instead, her parents had decided to homeschool her. Evelyn never forgave her parents for that. Not only had she missed out on all the normal teenage rites of passage that a regular high school affords, but she had also been an only-child. She'd never even had a sibling to confide in. She'd only had that pen pal in England (they'd met through an international pen-friends organization that Evelyn had found on a library bulletin board) and even then, the two of them hadn't started dishing the real dirt about their lives until they were grown up. Now as an adult, whenever she was around her parents, she would scream at them and use hardcore curse words and talk about sex, including her own sex life, as much and as raunchily as possible.

And I understood this. I was, after all, the author of the "Ireland: Land of Hardship, *Heartbreak*, and Pride" misfire. I understood her need to get back at her folks. I had much the same reaction to mine, who'd taught me that God was the Big Bigot-Prude in the sky—the one who was, on the one hand, out to get me and who, on the other hand, would be oh so happy to help me out if only I'd rejoin their religion and keep my zipper up. So, I could get with her hostility.

What I could *not* get with was her next complaint. She said that her mother had put on a French movie about a mentally impaired person and his caretaker. Pulling no punches, Evelyn flat-out said to me, "And I don't like retarded people, and I sure as shit don't want to watch a two-hour movie about one, so I was like, thanks for ruining my wind-down night, guys." I was speechless.

She'd run out of things to complain about, so she started dissing handicapped people? Imagine having to pay off that karma.

Evelyn ordered another cognac without asking if I'd like another beer, and then she told me to talk her down from her problems.

Well, although she had proven herself unworthy of it by slamming disabled people, she had come to the right guy for help. For months, I'd been steeping myself in self-help books, so I started tossing out some of the more innocuous phrases from them like: "This too shall pass" and "The darkest hour is always before the dawn," things I myself needed to hear. She went *pfft*. And then, maybe it was the alcohol talking, she proceeded to mock the patently gay voice and gay gesticulations I'd used when saying these things.

And that's when another phrase came to me—it's from *The Artist's Way*. It's in one of those sections where Julia Cameron tells us that we're likely to find the Morning Pages whispering to us things that we know in our hearts we ought to do but that we are avoiding doing. She said, for example, that our pages might tell us that we need to: "Dump [our] bitchy friend Alice."

Slagging mentally retarded people and mocking my gayness…

If I needed a last straw, either one of these things would have done.

It became clearer than ever that I needed to dump my bitchy former French teacher Evelyn. It'd certainly come up many a time in my Morning Pages and it was getting harder and harder to ignore.

And so, I stood up, threw down my beer money, and told Evelyn I never wanted to speak to her again. I walked out and went home.

And I never spoke to Evelyn again. I'd hang up on her when she'd call and then leave the phone off the hook. I'd erase her messages before I could even listen to them. Over the next few years, I'd see her on the street a few times. She looked better each time. She looked like she'd been to the gym. But I couldn't trust that these were anything more than cosmetic changes that she'd made to herself. She'd wave and stop to chat. But I wouldn't stop, and I wouldn't chat. I never spoke to Evelyn again.

❧

So now I was down to no friends.

And I was still working for Anne. And I was still going to St. Peter's and working in a soup kitchen on Saturday mornings. I also started volunteering at Literacy Chicago as an ESL tutor for a Mexican engineer and a Chinese laundromat attendant. The sex theater would be winding down its sex shows soon enough, so I'd have to find something else arts-related to do.

I was still dropping by Borders on my way home.

The self-help section was right next to the New Age section and the two sections often cross-fertilized. It's there that I found Ernest Holmes and Norman Vincent Peale and Wayne Dyer. I couldn't stand the Bible references in their books. The misogynistic, homophobic B-I-B-L-E is *not* the book for me. But I decided to look past those quotes. Peale was especially one for saying that if we thank God in advance for that new car or that new job we want, it will be ours with a bow on top, as long as we're strictly and strenuously positive in our thinking. Positivity wasn't exactly second nature for me, but I decided to give it a whirl.

It was after reading Peale and Holmes that I saw a job listing in the *Chicago Reader* for an entry-level position in the development department at the Art Institute of Chicago. How many hours had I spent in that museum, still using my student pass because it hadn't expired yet. I'd go there after work and on weekends and I'd moon over the impressionists and expressionists and the Ancient Greek and Roman sculptors. I'd make notes and go home and write highlights from my most recent visit to François, in my best French.

In my letters, I'd discuss the pointillism in Georges Seurat's *Un dimanche après-midi à l'Île de la Grande Jatte* and I'd tell him about how I'd play the soundtrack to Stephen Sondheim's *A Sunday in the Park with George* while viewing it. I told François about how I'd bought the soundtrack a few years before to remind myself of the moment when I first saw its original cast perform it on PBS's *American Playhouse*. It was 1988. Somebody had forgotten to turn the TV off in our kitchen before they'd left the house and I'd just happened to wander into the room. That's when I'd caught the opening scene, where Georges (Mandy Patinkin) begins to bring his painting to life: "White, a blank page or canvas. The challenge: bring order to the whole, through design, composition, tension, balance, light, and harmony." I was 14 with half my head shaved, scabby and surly as can be. I'd just gotten done slamming my body against my bedroom walls to Misfits' *Evillive* album. Now I was sitting at our kitchen table, spellbound by this Broadway musical. Seurat's life was full of anguish, penury, and romantic turmoil but, as I sat gaping at this exquisite production, I told myself that if all that suffering was the price of living of a life of imagination and expressiveness, then it was a price I was willing to pay. In my letter, I'd told François that the broadcast was one of the highlights of my life and that ever since, I'd been going back to the Art Institute incessantly just to luxuriate in the wonder of Seurat's creation. True, I'd since learned that penury was nothing to romanticize, and that anguish was no longer a land I wished to inhabit, but imagine being able to actually earn a living working in the same place that houses that painting!

The ad said that the Art Institute's development department needed someone with good writing skills. *A job where I could write!* I printed out my CV and, in my cover letter, I made it superabundantly clear why I was the man for the job:

Dear Sir or Madam:

Steps away from your doors, on Michigan Avenue, a Henry Arthur Dobson axiom stands engraved above the Fine Arts Building's archway: "All Passes, Art Alone Endures." I have always looked askance at these words. Art cannot endure *alone*. It requires institutions of the highest caliber to sustain it, and there is none higher than the Art Institute of Chicago. Herewith please find my résumé for the development-assistant position. As a writer and votary of the arts, I am eager to contribute all

my skills and talents to advancing the Art Institute's mission "to collect, care for, and interpret works of art across time, cultures, geographies, and identities, centering the vision of artists and makers."

I knew their mission statement because it was on a membership-renewal pamphlet that they'd sent me in the mail. I'd also been reading a book for job seekers that said that, in the body of our cover letters, we should cite the company's mission statement. That way, they'll see we've done our due diligence prior to applying.

Toward the end of the letter, I cited some words from Walter Pater to show that I was serious about art:

"The base of all artistic genius is the power of conceiving humanity in a new, striking, rejoicing way, of putting a happy world of its own creation in place of the meaner world of common days."

Riffing on Pater's quote, I ended by saying:

I look forward to helping the Art Institute, which showcases some of the most extraordinary works of artistic genius, usher in the "happy world" that this world so desperately needs.

I sent in the letter and waited on tenterhooks for their call. Following the advice of Peale and Holmes and Louise Hay and many other self-help authors, I started using affirmations. Many

times a day, I would write: "*I now have the job at the Art Institute.
I now have the job at the Art Institute.*" I sang these words in
front of my bathroom mirror each and every morning. I would
visualize myself writing reports in the Art Institute's development
office, and going into the museum on my lunch hour, and taking
free classes at its school since that's one of the perks of the job. I
would end by saying, "And so it is," and I'd thank the universe
for its largesse.

Peale's books were awash with examples of dreamers who went
for broke and came out on top. Such was their faith. You could
practically hear the pioneer horns blasting and the wagon wheels
creaking across the pages. According to Peale, these mavericks
knew that if they had a fallback plan—like "keep your current job
until something better comes along"—they'd only fall back.

And so, one Monday morning, under the spell of Peale, I
went for broke. After singing an extra refrain of affirmations in
my head, I walked into Anne's office and handed in my two-week's
notice. Anne intoned a long pause, then asked where I was going
to be working next. I told her I'd gotten a job writing for the
development department of the Art Institute of Chicago. ("Act
as if it's already happened," the books said.) Anne said that's good
because my talents were clearly not in being a legal secretary. My
only response was a smirk of victory.

It all but gave my mother a heart attack when I reported to
her that I'd done this, but she still managed to stay on this side of
life, maybe because the new novena she'd started for me had given
her the strength to carry on.

Over the next two weeks, when I wasn't going to St. Peter's and praying to the saints or going to Borders and reading about manifesting my destiny, or writing and singing affirmations in my apartment, or penning another letter to François, I was doing all the make-work I could do to make my last days at the for-profit hospital go faster. I was so eager to get on with things that I could barely stay in my skin. The Art Institute still hadn't called me in for an interview but that was okay. That's where faith comes in, I told myself, and I reminded myself that a lack of patience equates to a lack of faith.

I devised an elaborate directory so that Anne could easily find everything after I was gone. I showed it to her on my last day. She even complimented me on how much ingenuity I'd shown in putting it together—her first compliment, my last day.

Only, her eyes lasered right in on a possible discrepancy, "Shouldn't this line be under this heading?" she said about a certain contract (which technically went under the title "Agreement"). I said, "Well, that's a gray area. The contract straddles two areas of law."

She said, "Not in my book, it doesn't. It belongs in the opposite column. Change it and reprint it."

I did as I was told and came back with a printout of the corrected directory.

She checked my work and saw it was corrected satisfactorily. And she said, "Kyle, just do things right, okay? Your next boss might not be as understanding as I am."

At first, I spluttered but then I straight-up laughed in her face. She recoiled in horror at this feat of insubordination. "You mean there's someone out there who's even less understanding than you, Anne?" I said, "What a rotten, rotten world." Her mouth hung open, her chin hung down. And I don't know why exactly but in that moment, it struck me that Anne had a distinctly Irish chin. And this brought me back to that conversation that we'd had on my first day about our mutual heritage. I looked at the clock and saw it was time to sign off. And so I said, "See you at the next wake or funeral, Anne." And I thought about saying, "And I hope it's yours," but that seemed too mean-spirited and possibly even incriminating. What if she would somehow wind up dead by the end of the night? Anything's possible, and knowing her, I couldn't have been the only person she'd ever pissed off. I didn't want to be a suspect, so since I was being childish-impish anyway, I just opted for saying, "But not if I see you first," and I grabbed my black messenger bag and walked out.

Calling the world rotten, even sarcastically, was not the apogee of positive thinking. Norman Vincent Peale wouldn't have approved.

I'd hoped that expressing such negativity hadn't jinxed my chances of getting the new job that I'd been affirming I already had.

It did feel fucking great, though.

❦

So, I had my days free now.

And the days went by. And I waited for the phone to ring. I'd call the development office at the Art Institute, without giving my name. They said they were still rounding up applications.

I said to the universe, "Can you speed it up, please? I quit my job for this, you know!"

But then I'd go back to reading Peale and Holmes and Dyer whenever my faith would waver. I mused on how cool it was going to be to write to François about my big new gig, even though it was only entry-level. Maybe he'd fall in love with me. After all, by then, he could tell his friends in Paris that he's in a relationship with a *professional* American writer. We could officially call it a relationship then, couldn't we?

❦

It was coming on Christmas. The city had decked all its major streets and centers with balls of holly, lights, fir trees, mistletoes, and wreaths. I would see it all as I'd make my daily stop into St. Peter's, where I'd throw myself on the mercy of Whoever it is up there Who's running this show we're all in. I knew that the closer we got to Christmas and New Year's, the less likely it'd be that the Art Institute would be scheduling interviews for the position, and I needed to at least get a call for an interview if I was going to feel at all secure. I began to pray with all my might.

On Christmas Eve, I walked past the lady on the upturned milk crate. She was hugging the arms of her tattered ski coat. The stuffing and lining were peeking through the rips. A pink, Dollar-Store winter hat covered the top of her head and the tips of her ears. I slipped one of my last twenties, wrapped in a dollar bill, into her cup. She said, "Wait, wait. Stop for a second. *Stop.*" She handed me a card. A Christmas card, I supposed. I said a quick thank-you, smiled, and walked into the church. Once inside, I opened the envelope. It was a simple card, the kind you'd find at a Walgreens. There was a simple drawing of a simple Christmas tree that had simple red glass balls hanging from its branches. On the inside, she'd written me a note, "Thank you for helping to feed my family."

I choked up, but then buttoned up. I looked skyward and said, "And I'm even volunteering at a soup kitchen. C'mon! Give me the job! My name's written all over it."

I went home after saying my rosaries (never breathing a word about any of this to my mother, lest she think I'd rejoined the Church, so maybe I was only really being transparent with her about prurient things). As soon as I walked in the door, I reached over and picked up my Larousse French-English dictionary and grammar book from off my desk and went to the café around the corner from my apartment. I ordered a bottomless cup of coffee, brought it to a window table, rolled up my sleeves, and started my usual routine of conveying the secular version of the events of my life to François. I'd planned on writing to him all the way until suppertime.

Only, halfway down the first page, I suddenly stopped. I didn't know what it was that was stopping me, but I just stopped. I didn't feel I could go any further with the letter.

Now, you may be wondering: *How many letters had François written back to me, at this point?*

Well, none.

And suddenly that fact began to dawn on me. I had made such a sacred ritual of writing to him, but he had never once written back to me. I gave him all my deepest and darkest (while cleverly omitting references to St. Peter's and to prayer). But why? What was it all for? Did I really think he was interested? If he was, wouldn't he have written back to me by now?

And then another thing occurred to me…

In writing to François, I had started to become fascinated with my own life, just like I was when I'd write my Morning Pages, first thing every morning. True, I didn't have the life of a filmmaker who gets to jet off to every part of the globe. And I wasn't being lauded for any of my *projects* on French TV. Mine was the life of a working stiff, who was now unemployed, but who loved art and literature and film, and who had thoughts and opinions and a quivering heart, and who was also starting to see, through my daily letter writing, the artistic potential in the overlooked dramas of quotidian existence.

My life might not have seemed like much on the surface but when narrated with mindfulness (a word I'd learned from Jon Kabat-Zinn) and sensitivity (in French, no less) in my letters to François, I found that it could potentially be crafted into an exquisite, slice-of-life drama. It was almost as though I didn't need

François to even open my letters. They could have just sat there in the boxes that the concierge had brought out for him. It was enough to simply write them. Yes, François was attractive and accomplished, and yes, that's what had gotten me writing to him in the first place...

But now I had a new reason for writing these letters. I was falling in love with my own life. I started thinking that it was almost as if I didn't need to say "Cher François" at the start of my letters anymore. And I didn't even need to send them to him anymore. I'd sent him plenty already, and he'd never sent me a single one in return.

Maybe I could give up on him, I began to consider for the first time, and my life wouldn't be over. I wouldn't have a French lover to look forward to anymore, but I had something else. I had my own life. Be it ever so humble, maybe it was all I needed.

I crumpled up the letter I'd started writing him and put my French-English dictionary and French grammar book on the floor beside my messenger bag. I dug out my notebook, the one where I kept my Morning Pages, and I turned to a fresh page. Instead of writing "Cher François," I began with the same words with which I would begin each new round of Morning Pages. I wrote, in plain English, "Dear God," and I began to narrate the events of my day and the thoughts in my head, this time without any need to prove that I was clever or worldly or worthy.

⚘

I stopped writing to François in the evenings.
I started writing to God instead.

And in my letters, I swore and cursed and kicked and screamed. And it was all good. God would take me as I am. That's at least what *The Artist's Way* said. It's certainly not what the nuns or priests or schoolmarms at my Sunday school, grade school, and high school had told me. But *The Artist's Way* said to come as you are. So, I made a practice of telling it like it is with God. Julia Cameron, who was also raised Catholic, had given me a whole new way of having a relationship with the Divine. I was as difficult with God as Evelyn had been with Jim and Bob and her folks, but *The Artist's Way* said, "God can take it." I started to really enjoy the relationship.

⚘

Now, note that I said that I "almost" didn't need François.
As Jon Kabat-Zinn says in *Wherever You Go, There You Are*, "The mind has a mind of its own." And the mind does not let go lightly.

La douleur exquise didn't cease and desist simply because I'd stopped writing to François or told myself I didn't need him.

I still dreamed of the kisses we'd shared. In my head, those scenes in the bar and in the car were every bit as amorous and iconic as the one that Burt Lancaster and Deborah Kerr shared on the shores of Oahu in *From Here to Eternity*. Out of habit, I still checked my mailbox every day, but I also reminded myself each time that I wasn't going to find any letters from François in it.

And yet as I sang and wrote my affirmations for the job at the Art Institute, I was still in the habit of reminding myself that I knew François, who had an amazing job and worldly power, and I still hung on to his name like a talisman that could attract similar power into my own life.

Holding on is what the mind does, I was learning.

ℒ

New Year's Eve came. By now, I'd reconnected with my estranged best friend, the one who'd dumped me after I'd started sleeping with that guy John, the bi-curious jerk. We'd run into each other on the El one day after Christmas. I'd love to tell you that we talked everything out and made amends. The truth is, we just decided to sweep everything under the rug. It's not the healthiest resolution to a problem but it did bring us back together. I spent New Year's Eve with her and her fiancé. We sat in their living room and listened to Bowie's Berlin Trilogy, New York Dolls, and Lou Reed, and we caught up on lost time.

I had friends again.

My prayers were starting to work.

☞

I went to St. Peter's on New Year's Day.

I was running out of money, but I still gave some to the lady outside.

I've never been a fan of the Bible, but I will admit that it did cross my mind that there was something in it about two mites and how you'll reap a good harvest if you sow good seeds. I couldn't remember how exactly those passages went, but they went something like that.

I went into the church and I lit some candles. I prayed to Saint Mary for a favor, to Saint Anthony for help with finding the job at the Art Institute, and to Saint Jude, the patron saint of lost causes, so that he might also help me find that same job even if I was as hopeless as the Annes of the world thought me to be.

Now, it's not that I believed in the saints as anything *literal*. Who knows if most of them had even lived and breathed in the first place. I mean, back in the sixties, Pope Paul VI had to de-canonize hundreds of saints because it turned out many of them had never existed and that their biographies were based solely on folklore. Even if that were the case, though, I reasoned that God would still accept prayers said to saints from anyone, regardless of their religion or lack thereof, because the saints represent energies in the universe that are available to one and all. Catholics just happen to give those energies saints' names.

There was a Mass going on when I was in there that New Year's Day. In fact, it was a Holy Day of Obligation. But I didn't join in. I'd left the religion for life.

So, I just sat in one of the back pews, off to the side. I said a couple rosaries for the job and left before the Mass was finished. Maybe I'd sat through more than one Mass that day. I don't know. I wasn't paying any attention to what was happening on the altar.

෨

I continued doing my affirmations, just as Ernest Holmes's books had taught me. He told us to say declarative prayers. That's why you say, "I now have my dream job," even before you have it.

And I continued thanking God in advance for the job at the Art Institute, just as Norman Vincent Peale's books had taught me.

෨

And I called the development office again, three weeks into the new year.

I thought I'd given them enough time. It was too hard to bear, seeing that unblinking red light on my answering machine every day.

Back then, there wasn't any such thing as Caller I.D. I'd never left my name any of the times I'd called, so they didn't know which applicant I was, thank God.

That day, though, they told me the position had been filled.

All those affirmations, all those prayers, all those donations, all that community service, all those promises from Peale and company, and I'd never even gotten a call for an interview.

∅

I did not want to live. I broke down crying in my apartment all through the rest of January.

I still did my Morning Pages, and I still started with the words "Dear God," but just as a matter of routine. I was no longer writing to God at any other time of day.

And I sure as hell wasn't writing to François. What was I supposed to tell him, anyway? About what a loser I was for not getting the job? For not even getting an interview while he'd been off gadding about the Seven Wonders of the World—of which he was the Eighth?

I never read Norman Vincent Peale again. What a snake-oil salesman. And then years later, I'd learn that Peale crusaded against FDR's New Deal, blamed the poor for their poverty, officiated one of Trump's weddings after Trump's narcissism and lying and violence and numerous affairs had ended his previous marriage, and then I'd learned that Peale had even served as a spiritual advisor to the Trumps, preaching to them from the Prosperity Gospel, telling them all to think BIG, BIG, BIG as they grifted and grifted and grifted.

I never read Ernest Holmes again either.

I donated all those books to Goodwill. Not that I thought they'd do Goodwill shoppers much good. It might give them something to believe in for a little while, but only for a little while, I'd learned. I just wanted the books off my hands, is all.

I didn't go back to St. Peter's either. I regretted that that poor lady on the milk crate wasn't going to be getting my alms anymore. But I was done.

I did keep reading *The Artist's Way* and doing Morning Pages and Artist Dates. Anything to keep me writing, now that I wasn't writing to François.

♋

My mother would call to check in. She'd say she was either starting another novena or was in the middle of one for me and my job search. I told her to give her fingers a rest. It was no use. She said this setback didn't mean her prayers weren't working. She said the best was yet to come. Have faith.

She said she was also praying for my mental health. What was left of it.

♋

I didn't want to go back to temping. I told myself, you run into people like Anne that way. I was going to have to take whatever full-time, permanent job I could find if I were to avoid such a fate.

I had to ask my parents for money for the next month's rent, which sucked. But they happily gave it to me. I told them how ashamed I was to ask. And my father of all people, who normally had all the sensitivity of Archie Bunker (and who shared his politics), said there was no shame in it. He said, "I know you're looking for a job. And you're not a repeat offender at this unlike—"

and he mentioned the name of one of my siblings. I didn't relish him slamming this sibling, but I have to admit that it did feel good to not, for once, be the worst of us.

ℐ

I'd gotten a sliding scale therapist too. My folks said I needed one, and they said they'd pay for it. There was something subtly disqualifying in the offer. My parents were from the generation that thought that only crazy people need mental-health services. I knew they could use my seeking such services against me. I knew that, in any future disagreements that I might have with them, this could help them bolster their case that I shouldn't be taken seriously. After all, I'm the guy who sees a shrink, and I'd seen several before this[18].

In my late teens, my folks had expressed the hope that the therapist I was seeing at the time would help get whatever it was in my head that was telling me that I was gay out of my head once and for all. I was sure they were still holding out such hope when it came to this incoming shrink.

I didn't care. I needed one. I took them up on their offer.

The guy I found was good, and he was gay. (I didn't tell them that part, so that is one time I wasn't entirely transparent with them, along with all those times I didn't tell them I'd gone to St. Peter's and said rosaries.) He even gave me his cheapest rate. At the rate he'd given me, I could afford to take over payments once I got a job.

---

18 And I've seen a few since.

❧

I started writing to God again, outside of the Morning Pages, which I continued to do every morning and which I continue to do to this day.

I'd say, "I'm mad at you, but you're all I got in the end, and I can't make it through this life just on my own strength."

My Larousse French-English dictionary had started to gather dust, along with the grammar book.

I also started writing to God at night, entirely in English.

❧

Another month passed. I got a job. It was just another secretarial job, not a writing job, but at least it was full-time.

This time I was working at an ad agency, a startup. I gave the head of the company my leatherbound writer's portfolio. He read it and said, "This is excellent! But we don't have any writing jobs. But maybe as we grow..."

In the meantime, I was stuck answering phones again. At night, I would go home and try my hand at writing stories and essays.

A few people I'd gone to high school with were working at the agency. One was already the art director, one was a graphic designer, and one was an account representative. They were making a lot more money than I was, and unlike me, they were able to use their talents on the job. I got to watch as they moved on to bigger and bigger *projects*, and bigger roles in the company. I used to go to school with these people, and now I was taking their messages and bringing them coffee and sending their faxes and ordering in their luncheons. When they were with the boss or with a client, I'd tell whoever was calling for them, "He's in a meeting, may I take a message?" or "She's in a meeting, may I take a message?" And I consoled myself with the thought that maybe someday, someone, somewhere would tell somebody that I was in a meeting, but I had no idea when such a day would ever come or if it would ever come.

Every one of these former schoolmates had known Molly McGrory too, and a couple of them were still in touch with her. They knew that she and I had once been friends, so they'd stop by my desk with whatever news they had about her. One said that Molly was living with her fiancé in the South Loop. They were planning to wed that summer, but Molly had gotten a part in a festival called Glimmerglass, which was somewhere in upstate New York, so they'd pushed the wedding date back to October. I'd heard broadcasts from Glimmerglass on Classical 97. It seemed to be a big deal. Another one of the former schoolmates/current coworkers told me that Molly was already first understudy for the role of Marguerite in *The Damnation of Faust* at the Lyric Opera and that she had a real shot at seizing the role since the first-string mezzo-soprano had contractual difficulties, diva outbursts, and recurring laryngitis. To each of these highlight reels from Molly's life, I'd turn my palms up and say, "So she's doing well," and each time the phone, which it was my job to answer, would ring and I'd be saved by the bell.

However, on another occasion, there was no bell to save me when one of these coworkers also told me that they'd told Molly that we were all working together. I didn't ask what Molly's reaction was. I didn't ask whether Molly had mentioned to them that I had been working for Anne before this job, and I didn't ask if she might have mentioned to them what Anne's opinion of my work had been. I simply nodded. And in actual fact, I wasn't working *with* these former schoolmates; I was working *for* them. And I'm sure they'd told Molly as much. How could they not? How could you keep news like that a secret? And now that Molly knew where I was working, I saw that she could possibly even mention to Anne, the next time she'd see her, that I did not go on to write for the Art Institute after all. I was answering phones at an advertising agency. I'd only made a lateral move.

But the job paid my rent and bills, and it had adequate health and dental coverage, as well as two-weeks paid vacation.

As I said, I took what I could get.

⚘

François wrote back.

It took him five months, but he wrote to me.

The envelope arrived in the mail, five months after I'd sent my first letter and about two months after I had sent what I thought would be my last letter to him. It was a tissue-thin, pale-blue, *par avion* envelope that had vertical blue, white, and red stripes along the edges. It contained four postcards. He'd written on the backs of each of them in large handwriting. Each one had pictures of

Paris on the front—The Louvre, Le Jardin du Luxembourg, L'Arc de Triomphe, and *naturellement* Le Tour Eiffel. My guess was that he'd just stopped into a random pharmacy and bought a bunch and then he wrote on them and stuffed them in the envelope and sent it out just to get it off his plate.

He apologized for the delay. He said work had been *fou*. He told me not to despair over things like career: "You're young. You're still in the domain of the possible." I remembered he'd said those exact same words at Harry's Velvet Room. And on one postcard he'd written, "You're beautiful," and "Come see me in Paris." And he signed off, *{{Je t'embrasse.}}* ("I kiss you.")

Four postcards all in one envelope, all in large handwriting. Compared to how many thousands of soul-baring pages from me?

But I still wrote him back.

I only wrote a short letter this time, no longer than the one he'd written me. I told him I had a new job, that I was still only a secretary, a receptionist really, and that I'd go to Paris once I could take a vacation.

I didn't write anything to him about art or literature or film or any of those things.

I saved all that for my letters to God.

$\mathcal{L}$

My therapist asked me not to dwell on the brevity of François's letter...his postcards, rather.

I said, "He doesn't have any interest in me."

"He did ask you to visit him in Paris," the therapist said, "He did say he found you beautiful."

"The whole thing's too improbable," I said, "A documentary filmmaker in Paris, who's commissioned for projects all over the world, falling for a young American writer who's working a bottom-end job in Chicago?"

My shrink said, "Sounds like a great love story to me."

⌀

François did send me a follow-up letter months after that short one I'd sent him.

There were four postcards contained within this pale-blue, *par avion* envelope as well—this time with more French cities on them. One had a picture of Marseilles, another had one of Toulouse, another had a picture of Lyon, and the last one had a collage of Parisian scenes. Somehow, they all reminded me of when he'd said that he'd wanted to see Chicago ever since he was a little boy because he'd seen that one picture of its skyscrapers on a postcard.

What was the deal with François and postcards? I wondered.

Once again, his handwriting was large. He wrote it all in English. He started off by saying that he was just checking in this time. Work was still crazy, he said. He needs "loneliness," he said. (I think he meant solitude.) "Will you still come to Paris?" he said, "I kiss you,"

On the side of my job, I started volunteering for a European avant-garde theater in West Town that needed someone to write their grants and publicity.

It was like a whole other job. It didn't pay—the theater once had to throw a BYOB fundraiser, where they raffled off donated gift certificates and brought on hip-hop and punk bands to do benefit sets, just so they could pay their rent for the month—but I thought that writing their grants and publicity would help me pad my writer's portfolio and give me a leg up when it came to finding a paying writing gig.

And the people in this European avant-garde theater company were nuts. They drank a lot of wine after rehearsals, smoked dope, danced to world music, and there were always debauched Eastern Europeans from outside the company hanging around. They were either friends or friends of friends of the artistic director, who was Polish—well, Polish-American, really, but her parents and her sisters were born and raised in Poland and Polish was the first language she'd learned growing up, and it turned out she'd grown up in the next neighborhood over from the one where I'd grown up. She would go back to the motherland every summer and bring back obscure eastern European plays.

In addition, they'd stage plays by Genet, Brecht, Ionesco, and Stanislaw Witkiewicz, playwrights I admired in college, and the company would go all-out in their depictions of raw sexuality and harebrained societal absurdities.

By day, a lot of the company members were waiting tables, hawking newspapers on downtown sidewalks in the freezing cold, or temping just like I once did when I worked for Anne. Many of them were constantly getting fired. But these were theater people. They didn't judge each other for it.

I loved them.

✍

Eight months after I started my job at the ad agency, I was eligible to take a vacation.

I wrote to François and proposed the dates for my arrival. And then he called me from Paris. We actually spoke on the phone. Mostly in English this time.

"I've been reading your letters, the ones you sent me months ago" he said, "You write good French."

I said, "No. No, I don't. *Ma grammaire est atroce.*"

He said, "*Non, non.* We understand you. I read them to my friends. I hope you don't mind. There is great *éloquence.* A delight to read them."

I thanked him and told him I'd go ahead and book a ticket to go see him.

He said, "*Super!* Just write to me the time. And should I carry a sign at the airport? One that says, 'Allo, Kyle! I am François.'"

I laughed and said, "No, no. I'll never forget what you look like François."

François said, "I kiss you." He said it in English.

❧

I spent the night before my flight moving into a new apartment on the north side, right on the shores of Lake Michigan. Actually, it was a condo that belonged to friends of my parents. Their son was moving out of it, and they were letting me rent it for only $400 a month.

I spent all night moving into it and returned the U-Haul when the depot opened first thing in the morning. Then I went back to the new place, showered, and had just enough time to grab a cab to O'Hare airport. I barely made my flight, a flight to Cleveland that connected to a later flight to Paris.

I landed at Charles de Gaulle the next morning. I got off the plane and claimed my bags.

I looked out and saw a sea of placards with all sorts of people's names on them.

I scanned all the faces. Nobody who looked the way I'd remembered François looking was there. And he hadn't sent me any pictures of himself in the mail, and I hadn't sent him any of me. I wandered around the area for a whole hour. I couldn't find him.

He'd given me his cell-phone number, but I didn't have a cell phone myself and wouldn't for another five years.

I went to a pay phone and tried calling him. But the phones were weird. I wasn't dialing right, it seemed. I was missing a city code or a country code or some kind of code. I didn't know which. But I was missing something. I couldn't complete the call.

I walked around the area some more. I still saw no-one who looked like I remembered him looking.

Eventually, I decided to grab a cab and go to his apartment in the 14th arrondissement.

ℊ

I found his name on his building directory and rang the buzzer.

No answer.

A stout ruddy-faced old man in overalls, who presumably lived in the building, asked if he could help. I showed him François's name and address. He wanted to help me solve the problem, but he did not understand my French and ended up doing what I'd just done, except he was making a mortifying display of it. He kept *leaning* on to the buzzer. And I mean, he would not stop.

If François had been home to hear this man laying on the buzzer, I would have considered flagging down a cab and going back to the airport to ask for the next flight out.

But François wasn't home.

I chuckled and told the well-intentioned oaf that it was okay. I would take it from here. He could go on with his day. He wandered off in a doddering daze.

That's when a little boy and a cross-eyed little girl in spectacles came up to me. They kept asking me, in French, what I was doing there. I smiled and said, {{*Je cherche mon ami*}}. They laughed at my French and laughed at my accent, and they kept trying to get me to say more words so that they could laugh at me, Monsieur

Funny Talk, some more. But they were little scamps, like my nephews back in Chicago, so I didn't take it to heart. I just pulled a funny face and gave them a goofy grin.

Then I pulled up the lever on my suitcase and wheeled it to the end of the street. The little boy and girl chased me and mocked me, but I just laughed along with them. Their mother soon came running up behind us. She caught them both by their hands and scolded them. She kept saying to me, *{{Ooo, je suis desolée, monsieur.}}*

I smiled and said, *{{C'est pas grâve.}}*

She scolded the children some more and pulled them up by their wrists as she marched them back to their home. They kept looking back at me, and I waved and gave them another funny face and goofy grin. I rounded the corner and never saw them again.

I wheeled my suitcase through the neighborhood until I found a pension about seven streets away. I booked a room, so I could shower and chill out while I tried to figure out where François was.

I was so jetlagged, though, and so exhausted from the move the previous day that I fell dead asleep on the bed right after my shower.

It was nighttime by the time I woke up.

I scrambled back downstairs with my luggage and ran back to François's building.

Thank God he answered his buzzer this time. *{{Ah, Kyle!}}* he said over the speaker, and he told me which apartment to go to and buzzed me up.

I tore up to his door, lugging my suitcase bump by bump up each stair in his stairwell. I was huffing and puffing as I knocked. He opened the door. "Kyle!" he said and scooped me into a hug.

François was as fit as I remembered him being. His hair of black lamb's wool was still short and cropped and slightly graying; his summer sweater clung tightly to his chest, the sleeves rolled up to expose his tawny arms. His skin was still tight around the cheekbones and jaw, ascending to his chestnut eyes. It was worth all the hullaballoo just to be here in his arms again.

He said, "What happened?"

Struggling to breathe, I said, "I couldn't find you at, at, at the airport. Now I wish I hadn't told you not to carry that sign. I'm, I'm so sorry, François. So sorry."

He said, "I was there. I took off the day. I went to the airport. I waited around. I looked for you. I checked with the airlines. They had a record of your arrival. I went to customs. They said you'd gotten past customs. I looked. I looked. And I got up early. I'd made all this food," he motioned to a whole spread of niçoise salad and bread and fruit and wine.

I said, "Oh, awesome! You have food! Great! Great! I'm starving. Thank you."

"Well, yes," he said, "Have some. But I lose the day, Kyle."

"I'm sorry, François," I said, "I really am. It's just I, I tried to call and…Is that *quiche des légumes?*"

He said, "Yes, it is…Go. 'Ave some."

I said, "Thanks, don't mind if I do." I grabbed a plate and started putting the quiche on it.

François said, "But what number did you call?"

I said, "This one," and I took the number out of my pocket.

He said, {{*Oui, c'est…mon numéro de téléphone.*}} He walked over to his landline and dialed. His cell phone rang. He hung up and dialed again. His cell phone rang again. François gave me a look of incredulity.

I took a bite of the quiche and said, "I promise you, François, I tried. But it didn't work for me when I dialed. And I'm so, so sorry. But I'm here. I'm here."

François took a deep breath and said, "Yes, you are here and that is what is important." He turned around, poured me a glass of red wine, and brought it to me. He gave me a deep kiss. I felt absolved.

He brought me over to the couch. I looked around. I don't know why but in my head, I'd built up the image of François living like Sardanapalus in the Delacroix painting—in a lair that's all tricked out with Second Empire furnishings and trappings, or at least with a fine leather chaise lounge. But no. His apartment was clean but spare, like mine. I supposed it was because he was on the road so much, but wouldn't that be all the more reason to do the place up, so he could have something warm and cozy to come home to? Unlike me, he had the money for it. Or it could be, like me, it wasn't important to him how his own place looked. Maybe, like me, he was that anomaly among gay men: the kind born without any interior-design talent. His couch was a futon, like mine, but with a saffron Indian kantha throw covering it. That was a nice touch. I made a note to buy one on Devon Avenue when I got back to Chicago.

François poured himself a glass of wine and sat down with me. We held hands and talked, in English, about his projects. He said he'd been all over Africa, mostly covering emerging infrastructure-reform initiatives in its various nations. He was documenting how China was pouring money into the continent. His *émissions* speculated on what affect this could have over indigenous cultures and the integrity of the land. They also explored how homeopathic remedies were having a positive effect on various health crises; however, they also covered the reality of how AIDS was rampant in Africa, how certain regimes were seizing vital medications, and how plethoric superstitions were influencing people to refuse prophylactics, as well as medications approved by the FDA and its international equivalents. Instead, some people were falling for chicanery that said, for example, that putting a condom over a special totem pole outside your hut, instead of wearing it, would prevent STD transmission. (Who was I to judge? At one point, I'd believed the things in Norman Vincent Peale's books.) They covered protest efforts against female genital mutilation, and also addressed how vigilante groups of women had formed to protect young girls and infants from sexual assault now that a notion had caught fire that having sex with a virgin could cure your AIDS.

He'd also met with sangomas and shamans and healers and medicine men and village witches. He said that in Togo, one of the medicine men had cast the bones and read them for him. The medicine man told him that a blonde woman would be coming into his life and that she would make him very happy. We both laughed. He stroked my hair and said, "You are blond, Kyle. *Un peu roux, mais un blond foné.*" I said, "I'm not a woman." He said he knew that, but there was only so much the medicine man could say without getting anyone in trouble with the law. He asked me if I was still writing. I said I was trying to. He said he loved my letters. He said he'd even reread them sometimes.

We talked for a little over an hour, but it was getting late, so we went to bed. His bedroom had a classic view of the rooftops of Paris. It was right over Cimetière du Montparnasse as well, where he reminded me that Baudelaire was buried. I said that while it's true that Baudelaire had written "Litany to Satan," he'd also asked to have the last rites of the Church performed over him on his deathbed. François shrugged and said, {{Un Catholique typique!}} I asked him if Honoré de Balzac was buried there too. I've always loved Balzac, especially for how he'd been a failed student. François took his shirt off, exposing a thin but firm frame so unlike Balzac's. He walked up to me slowly, kissed my forehead, and said, {{Non, mon cher, Balzac est enterré au Père Lachaise.}}

We kissed and fell back into bed. And this time we did make love. We made up for that missed opportunity on the night we met. And it was sweet, and it was hot, and we laughed when we were finished, and he said it was adorable how I'd sent him all those letters, and we flirted well into the twilight. We fell asleep in each other's arms.

François woke up for work the next morning. And I did my Morning Pages and looked forward to the week ahead.

ॐ

The second day, I decided to go all the way out to Père Lachaise to put a few roses on Balzac's grave. Later that day, I came back and before heading up to François's apartment, I put a few more on Sartre and Beauvoir's tomb in Montparnasse Cemetery. That's where they're buried together, even though they were never man and wife. They did not believe in marriage. To them, it was a stultifying bourgeois institution. They deplored institutions. It's why Sartre had refused the Nobel Prize. He said, "I don't want to become an institution." He wanted to be free of all that. Sartre and Beauvoir never even lived together. They made sure to live across the street from each other, though, and they would write together every morning at Deux Magots, unless one of them had been called away by another lover or a lecture engagement or the war. Simone de Beauvoir was also buried wearing the ring that Nelson Algren, a Chicago author, had put on her finger. Beauvoir had even thought of moving to Chicago to be with Algren, but she'd quit him because she couldn't bring herself to quit Sartre.

People had left lipstick kisses on their tombstone. Others had set down metro tickets and put rocks on top of them. One woman came up behind me and put hers down too. I asked her why there were so many metro tickets. She said that people write little notes to Sartre and Beauvoir (mostly to Beauvoir, she's better liked) on them and they put rocks on top so they won't scatter to the wind. I found that so sweet. To this day, I don't know what the New York equivalent would be.

I'd have to see how things would go, but I thought if all went well, maybe François and I could share a tomb someday. After all, Beauvoir had fallen for a Chicago author. True, she'd let him go but she did go down wearing his ring. If there had once been a Beauvoir and Algren, why couldn't there be a François and Kyle? And couldn't our union last where Beauvoir and Algren's hadn't? Anything could happen in this world, especially good things. That's what a lot of the self-help books I'd read had said, and they weren't all bullshit.

I had six more roses. I went back to François's apartment and put them in an empty vase that I'd found in a cabinet above his kitchen sink. I set them out for him on his living-room coffee table for when he'd come home from work.

ℒ

In the mornings, while I'd be meditating, François would leave on the kitchen table the addresses of wherever I was supposed to meet him after he got off work. Each night, he told me, we were going to be having dinner with different friends of his.

I'd never met these friends before, of course, but they'd give me *mwha-mwha*, two-cheek kisses instead of simply shaking hands upon introduction. Continental manners. If only Americans were so chic with strangers.

Yet something had changed *tout à coup* between François and me. At dinner, he started ignoring me. Not only would he neglect to include me in discussions, which he and his friends conducted solely in French, but he would coldly turn his face to me.

I would catch keywords they were saying, and I'd try to keep up, but when I would attempt to address anyone or everyone in French, they would look at me like I was not only speaking a language they did not understand, but like I was speaking a vile, revolting tongue that they hoped to never hear again.

When François would address me in front of them in English, he would say something on the order of, "Why don't you go to London while you are in Europe, Kyle? It's right across the English Channel, you know. It's easy to get to. And there, you speak the language."

After enough of this, I stopped biting my tongue. I finally said to him, "I know where London is, François. But I came here to be with you."

He crossed his arms and looked away.

I thought he must still be sore about the mix-up at the airport. Yes, the first night had ended well enough, but maybe he hadn't completely accepted my apology and maybe the memory of what had happened was still getting to him. I didn't say anything about it right away, and I wasn't going to say anything about it in front of his friends.

After dinner, François and I went back to his place. He looked at but did not comment on the half a dozen roses I'd arranged for him in the vase. As we got ready for bed, I brought out a French translation of *Leaves of Grass*[19] that I'd bought for him from a *librairie* that I'd found near the Place de Pigalle. We got into bed,

---

19   *{{Feuilles d'Herbe}}*

and I tried to read to him from *Calamus* in French. By the time I reached the third selection, he ripped the book out of my hands and said, "I will read it," and he did, to himself, silently. Only then would he acknowledge that Whitman was a good poet. And he turned out the light and closed his eyes. François fell asleep. I didn't. And it was only partly because I was still battling jetlag.

As I lay next to François, it was not lost on me that the poem he'd stopped me from reading is called "Sometimes with One I Love."[20] It ends in the parenthetical verse:

(I loved a certain person ardently and my love was not return'd,
Yet out of that I have written these songs.)[21]

𝔰

B y day three, I couldn't avoid the subject of the crossed wires at the airport any longer.

I brought it up to him in his living room after dinner, another dinner where he and his friends had once again frozen me out.

He said, "It's not the *aéroport*, Kyle. It's...*you*. You know, I used to read your letters. I used to read them to my friends. And they were beautiful. I mean, the *grammaire* was a little *problématique*. But we understand. We know what you were saying. But then you speak and it's...it's...not good."

---

20   French translation: {{*Parfois Celui que J'aime*}}
21   French translation: {{(*J'ai aimé ardemment une certaine personne et mon amour n'a pas été rendu/Pourtant c'est à partir de cela que j'ai écrit ces chansons.)*}}

"Well," I shrugged, "Obviously, I'm no Charles de Gaulle. But you're not exactly Winston Churchill when it comes to English, François."

"*D'Accord.* I know. But tell me. Why is it so bad? You spoke so well when I met you the first time in Chicago."

"Well, I wasn't long out of school then," I said, "Now I'm further out. I don't have people to practice with. I don't talk to that woman anymore, the one you met, the one who was with Lucien. She used to be my French teacher in college. But now I'm out of college. And language classes are expensive. At least for me they are. I don't have a great job. I don't make a lot of money."

"*Et violà!*" is all he said, and he stood up and went to the bedroom and started getting ready for bed.

I told him I was going out. He said, *{{D'accord, bonne nuit.}}*

I picked up my black messenger bag, went out, and walked aimlessly around afterhours Paris. I'd stop into whatever all-night brassieres I could find, order a cup of chamomile tea, and write to God in my notebook. In one dive near the stairs to Montmartre, I wrote something like:

The game's up, God. François's got me pegged. My French was never as good as I made it out to be in my letters and neither am I. Writing him all that highfalutin crap in French, what was I thinking? But the thing is, I meant what I was saying. Or I thought I meant it. Maybe I was too aspirational. I mean, shit, writing about all those lofty subjects, in all that lofty language, to someone so out of my league? Did I learn nothing from Icarus? Clearly not. I mean, look at the sentence

I just wrote. I mean, who the fuck, in this day and age, even thinks of referencing Icarus? But as long as we're on the subject, will I ever, ever learn to come down to earth before the sun melts my wings? Or before I'm shot out of the sky? How the hell could I have gotten through life in an Irish family without ever learning that one supreme lesson, the one thing they ever tried to teach me: "Know your place"? How could I have never learned that lesson? No wonder I almost flunked out of high school.

I asked for strength and for guidance on what to do next. And I got up, tipped the waiter, and walked around nocturnal Paris some more.

When I got back to François's apartment at about 4 a.m., I crawled into bed next to him.

He said hello to me the next morning in the living room, but I was doing my Morning Pages, so I simply waved.

When I was done with my pages, I walked into the bedroom, folded the pillow I'd slept on in half, and sat down to meditate on the bed. I was exhausted from having had little, if any, sleep. Plus, I was still jetlagged, so I kept nodding off. When the timer on my watch beeped to signal the end of my meditation session, I uncrossed my legs and wandered into the rest of François's apartment, yawning.

François had left for work.

But he'd left me a note on the kitchen table. I thought it might be an apology. I felt like I owed him an apology too, for ever getting above myself like I did in my letters.

Instead, his note was telling me that we were meeting some other friends of his for dinner at another restaurant. He left the place's name and address.

Another dinner?, I said to myself. With more of his friends? His *beau monde* friends? The ones who'd scowl when I would try to speak to them in French? Would François bring up London again? Was he counting down the days to my departure? Is this what he'd been telling them all in his rapid-fire French as I'd sit there looking on like a dunce?

Another, more confident part of me stepped forward and all diffidence disappeared. I went back to his bedroom and packed my suitcase. I left a note saying that it was incredibly rude of him to criticize my French like he did, and that I didn't come to Paris just to be told to go to London.

And then I lied...

I said, "Last night I went to a bar in Le Marais and met a guy named Pierre[22]. I'm going to spend the rest of my time in Paris with him. Pierre *wants* me to be here."

I left his keys on his kitchen table and left without locking the door. (You couldn't lock it without keys, after all.) I checked back into the pension I'd found the first day and spent the rest of my trip walking through the Louvre and the Musée D'Orsay and the Picasso Museum, hoping not to be found. And I wasn't.

I didn't have an email address. He didn't have my new phone number in Chicago, and I hadn't given the phone company

---

22   I recently recounted this part of the story to Julius. Julius said, "Really, Kyle? *Pierre*? Couldn't you have gone with something more convincing like... Loïc?"—Told ya I wasn't a good liar.

permission to give out my new number on their "no longer in service" recording. And if he'd bothered to write me a poison pen letter or even an apology postcard, it would have been returned to sender because for several months after I'd gotten back, I'd failed to sign a change-of-address card at the post office to have my mail forwarded.

⊘

There was news when I got back to Chicago.

The head of the company called me in. He said he wouldn't be able to farm in the proofreading and copywriting work that he'd hoped to give me. He couldn't create the writer position for me.

And he said he didn't want to box me into a receptionist job since that's not what I wanted to do long-term.

He advised me to look elsewhere for work and said that he'd tell the Department of Labor that I didn't quit, I was fired, so I could collect unemployment.

With that, I started a full-time internship with the theater and lived off unemployment checks. Eventually, I made some commission from the grants I started bringing in, but in the meantime, the artistic director would have me over for dinner so I could save money on food.

I ended up tripling the theater's annual revenue within seven months. That still wasn't nearly enough to give me a salaried position with them, but it gave me a grants-and-publicity portfolio that got me a full-time job writing for a civil-rights organization.

And I kept writing grants and publicity for the theater at night too.

How could I not?

This highly unprofessional, ragtag lot ended up getting me my start as a professional writer.

And they were all such freaks.

I loved them.

℘

As for François, this didn't turn out to be the last I ever saw of him.

You see, a couple more years went by, and I kept on writing essays and stories, and I also started writing plays. And I was reading too much Hemingway, so I decided to move to Paris.

I saved a bit, quit the job I had at the civil-rights organization, gave up my apartment, and bought a one-way ticket[23].

And it was a fool's errand. I didn't know how to set down roots, so I started vagabonding all over Europe until I had the oh so bright idea to move to New York, flat-broke.

But that's another story.

Let's just say, I had to write to God all the time to survive the ordeal.

---

23   This was pre-9/11 when you could still buy a one-way ticket to a European country without getting grilled at either your departure or arrival points. They didn't even check my passport upon arrival at Charles de Gaulle. Those days are over and they're never coming back.

But getting back to my stint in Paris, I have no idea what I did with the napkin that had François's address and phone number on it. I never took it out of my copy of *Hopscotch*, but I think I might have given that book away to the resale shop at Howard Brown Health Center, an AIDS charity in Chicago. I'd given them most of my books before I made the move to Paris and then to New York, so *Hopscotch* and the napkin were probably in the pile with the other books.

Now, what I did hang on to was the card from the pension where I'd stayed on that fateful trip to see François. And I decided that's where I'd stay again until I'd get settled. The pension was only a short stroll from François's apartment, but I figured Paris was a big enough city for us to never cross paths again.

About two weeks into my stay, though, I was walking past Place de La Nation. I stopped at a crosswalk and waited for the little white figure to tell me I could go ahead and walk. I looked to my right, and a little distance away, I saw a familiar face. There was François, heading my way amid a sea of other pedestrians. He was carrying some film equipment. He recognized me. He looked as though he was coming up to talk to me.

The little white walking figure appeared on the crosswalk screen. I gave François a glower and moved on.

Whether or not he tailed me, I do not know.

All I know is that I did not look back.

I did stop at a brasserie about a mile ahead, though. And I took out my notebook and wrote: "Dear God, For all François knows, I'm still with Pierre." Now, the nuns and priests had taught me that God doesn't like it when you fib like I did in my Dear

John letter to François, but then again, Julia Cameron does say in her books that God has a sense of humor.

This story doesn't even end there.

Julius and I have been to Paris together many, many times since my failed attempt at living there. And as I said at the beginning of this book, I might get another chance to live there if a certain deal goes through at Julius's job.

I'm not sure it's the best idea, though, given how Paris is one of the cities that's being hit the worst, at least in Europe, with heat waves in this age of climate catastrophes. But who knows what other regions could get hit even worse than Paris in the coming years. It could be New York, for all we know. After all, a couple years ago, streetcar cables were melting in the heat in Portland, Oregon. That'd never happened before, and that used to be a town where the rain never stopped. Maybe the days of wine and roses are over, and we've all reached the end of the line, and nobody should ever again be thinking about how lovely it would be to live in Paris or anywhere else. Maybe the best we all can do now is hunker down and get used to each successive wave of floods, draughts, and fires. I hope that's not true, but many great minds are saying it is. I'll remain agonistic on whether we've all had our last waltz. We'll have to see what happens next.

Climate catastrophes aside, Julius says that he might like to live in Paris for a time, though he also says he doesn't think he'll ever be able to live anywhere but New York over the long haul. New York is his city, he says. He says he wants to die in New York. That's always where he goes to: his death.

Not that it's a bad thing to remember death. Every morning, right after I do my Morning Pages, I recite the Five Remembrances[24] of the Buddha to remind myself of our fragility and mortality. The third Remembrance is: "I am going to die. There is no way to escape death." The first Remembrance also hits home as I inch up to my fiftieth birthday: "I am subject to aging. There is no way to escape aging." Unlike Norman Vincent Peale's books, the Remembrances are designed to give us a reality check. They remind us of who and what are truly important in our lives, and of how little time we have left with them, even in the best-case scenarios.

Back in the eighties, when Julius was a student at Georgetown, he'd studied for a whole year at the Sorbonne. He'd taken French literature classes from the time he was a little boy, educated at Jesuits schools in San Juan. He's fluent in French and, unlike François, he's infinitely patient with the fact that I am not.

Now, that's not to say that Julius doesn't lose his patience with me over other things.

For instance, on one of our trips to Paris, this must have been ten years ago, Julius came up with a brilliant plan. To save on museum fees, he'd bought us special tourist passes, issued by the French government. You could just flash your pass and get into any museum in the city. You didn't have to wait in line for tickets and you got to go through express lanes for exhibits.

---

24   The Five Remembrances in Buddhism are as follows: (1) I am subject to aging. There is no way to escape aging. (2) I am subject to ill health. There is no way to escape illness. (3) I am going to die. There is no way to escape death. (4) Everyone and everything I love will change, and I will be separated from them. (5) My actions are my only real possessions, and I cannot avoid their consequences. My actions are the ground upon which I stand.

After we'd checked into our Airbnb in St. Germain des Prés, I stuck my pass in the left front pocket of my jeans, where I keep my iPhone. I did that for the next couple days too.

One afternoon, Julius went off to see several museums, and I stayed nearby our Airbnb so I could write at Deux Magots.

Julius texted me to meet him for a late lunch at Maison Blanche. When I got on the metro, I pulled out my phone to tell him I was on my way. Yet my left front pocket felt lighter than before. I put my hand in and couldn't find the government-issued museum pass. It must have fallen out on one of the times that I'd pulled out my phone. And unfortunately, I'd already hit dial on that same phone and Julius answered, and I had to tell him what had happened.

Julius gave me the tongue-lashing of all time for my blundering. Feeling cornered and obtuse, I barked back, and it soon became a contest of who could out-bark the other. What ensued were a lot of hang-ups and callbacks and don't-you-hang-up-on-me's and other forms of unproductive marital reprisals.

Yet then I remembered the Five Remembrances of the Buddha. The fourth is "Everyone and everything I love will change, and I will be separated from them." The Fourth Remembrance helped me to see the folly in this fight we were having. Far better to regroup and seek peace.

"We have the order number," I said when we finally started addressing the actual bone of contention, "We can get the pass replaced."

He said, "It's all red tape here. They're all, what do they call those bureaucrats in England?"

I said, "Jobsworths?"

He said, "Jobsworths. Do you think anyone here is going to stick their neck out for us?"

I said I'd scour the streets of St. Germain des Prés. He said it was hopeless. I said it wasn't and I left the metro station and retraced all my steps. I eventually came around to sharing his pessimism, though. I'd combed every inch of pulverized concrete on Boulevard St. Germain but could not detect a lost museum pass.

Julius wasn't the only one I had to contend with about this issue either. I was bracing myself for another internal assault from my inner critic, the one who calls my ADD diagnosis a lame excuse for my absentmindedness and stunning lack of character. My inner critic is more brutal and vicious than the worst schoolyard bully. A Buddhist teacher I know suggests that we give our inner critic a name, so that it becomes more identifiable and less omnipotent. I'd started calling mine Anne, after my dear old boss. It was also my late father's stepmother's name. My own internal Anne is an Irish hellion with Anne's flaming red hair and funereal face. It started in on me that day in Paris, *"Can't you get anything right? Ever?"* And I just said, "Oh, hello, Anne. Good to see you again." Now that I'd miniaturized her to a name, Anne the inner critic took flight and evaporated.

Having vanquished Anne, I steeled myself for the next over-the-phone Donnybrook with Julius. He is a Scorpio, after all, and I'm a Taurus, so we're at opposite ends of the zodiac, which can lead to the Clash of the Titans. But before I could call him, his number flashed on my screen. I picked up his call with a sigh and prepared to hear yet again about how I'd messed everything up.

But there was no need.

Julius said that this time he was calling to tell me that he'd just gotten off the phone with the French Jobsworths and that they'd told him that they could replace my card at any time, now that he'd given them the order number. Their offices were right near the Eiffel Tower, which is a short stroll from Maison Blanche. He said he was already on his way to pick it up and that he'd see me at the restaurant.

I went back into the metro station and took the train over.

By the time I got to Maison Blanche, Julius was already seated and enjoying a glass of burgundy. I waved to him. Julius took his earphones out and gave me a broad smile. He handed me my replacement pass. This time, I made sure to put it in my *back* pocket.

I sat down and asked him how his day had been, aside from the museum-pass debacle.

Julius said, "You know, after I picked up the replacement pass, I went and sat under the Eiffel Tower. It's something I used to do when I was a student here. I used to sit under the Eiffel Tower and take out my Walkman and listen to a cassette tape that I had of Maurice Revel's *Boléro*. My grandfather used to love that piece, and it always reminds me of him. Do you know *Boléro*?"

"Yes," I said, "I know *Boléro*." And I didn't mention anything about the time Anne sat on the other side of my desk and clicked invisible castanets. I didn't mention anything about Bo Derek or Leonard Maltin or Classical 97 FM or the constant invocations of the ghost of Molly McGrory that I was treated to. I didn't mention the letters to François or anything else about those days. I just let Julius continue his stroll down Memory Lane. His seemed to be so much more primrose than mine.

But Julius said, "I used to get my heart broken a lot in those days, when I'd first started sitting under the Eiffel Tower and listening to Ravel. And I just assumed that that's how it would be for me until I died. I was so fatalistic. I mean, you know me. I've always had this obsession with death. And I've always had this obsession about what my life will be like when I'm old."

I said, "I know, you're always pitching your tent right on death's front porch."

Julius said, "Yes, but I was even more fatalistic when I was, say, in my twenties and thirties. I'd just assumed that love was always over in the morning. And I'd look into the future, and I'd see myself at the age I am now. And I'd actually *see* myself listening to Revel's *Boléro*, all alone under the Eiffel Tower. And I'd see myself just…going off all by myself once the last notes of the tape would sound. And it'd be just me walking off. No partner, no husband. Well, no man had a husband in those days, not *legally* anyway, but you know what I mean. I thought I'd never meet my partner. I'd resigned myself to it being just…me alone, trying to keep myself busy so I wouldn't feel so lonely.—But you see, that's *not* my life. I see that now. And it's because I have you."

Julius put his hand over mine. And I put my hand over Julius's. We both stargazed into each other's eyes.

"Yes" I said, "And that's why you shouldn't get so mad at me when I lose a museum pass."

Kyle Thomas Smith
June 2023
New York, NY

ACKNOWLEDGEMENTS

Deep, deep gratitude to all who helped me during the creation and completion of this book. These names include Aaron Kass, Geoff Weiss, Sébastien de Féraudy, Caitlin Myer, Xiaoyan Zhang, Victor Melenhorst, Jennifer Harris, Martin Aylward, Jill Dearman (editor extraordinaire), Benjamin McEvoy, Hogarth Brown, and of course my deepest gratitude to Julius Leiman-Carbia, without whom there would have been no happy ending (take that as you will).

ABOUT THE AUTHOR

Kyle Thomas Smith is the author of the multi-award-winning books *85A* and *Cockloft: Scenes from a Gay Marriage*. He lives in New York City with his husband and cats.

You can email him at shugakyle@yahoo.com – an awful email address from the nineties that hasn't gone away.